UNLOCKING "SECRET" OBSTACLES IN THE SOUTH

ED Graves

BALBOA.PRESS
A DIVISION OF HAY HOUSE

Balboa Press books may be ordered through booksellers or by contacting:

Balboa Press
A Division of Hay House
1663 Liberty Drive
Bloomington, IN 47403
www.balboapress.com
844-682-1282

Print information available on the last page.

ISBN: 978-1-9822-7302-6 (sc)
ISBN: 978-1-9822-7303-3 (e)

Balboa Press rev. date: 08/13/2021

CONTENTS

ACKNOWLEDGEMENTS

I would initially like to honor and acknowledge my pastor of First Nazareth Baptist Church at Millwood and Gervais Street in Columbia SC. Pastor Blakely Scott. I have developed wonderful and loving relationships with Rev. Doris Jumper, to whom I refer to as my sister. Rev. John Richardson a good friend. And then there is my eleventh grade high school teacher, a beautiful lady that we use to call the pretty "red Bone" and most of all the cool "black cat" who managed to win her heart in marriage, Mrs. Amy Johnson Jackson and husband "Jack". My friend Samson and wife, Harrison "cool" Reardon and bride. Blanche McRrant and "Mac" Macfadden, Prentice Moore, Bonnie and Bernetta. A great friend and fellow athlete Ishmael Prealeau. The famous Eula Thurmond and Amelia Owens. Cynthia Clark, Arlinda L. Johnson, beautiful "JO" Jo Ann Pyles, cute Barbara David, Famous athlete Jimmy Floyd and a great coach Harry Jeter whom I sincerely took great pleasure and enjoyment in just whipping the daylights out of in Tennis. And then there's Queen Ester and Mayvern, Joe Bethea, Dean Bell and my sister Dr. Alma Byrd. Special recognition to my Grandsons Curtis Tillman, Tevan Scott and my Nephew Trey Reaves. Minnie Bele Crawford, who married the most famous baseball pitcher in the Nation but never got his chance to show his stuff. Collin Moore, Grandson of Wanda and Edgar Moore. Glendora Pee-but then there's Addie Pee Cain.

INTRODUCTION

What does it mean today, to be free and black in America? Home, where ever one lives is about memories, sights and sounds, thoughts and feelings of the past and present.

No school in America taught us anything about the 1ST and 2ND Union Military Black Civil war Regiments from South Carolina, who not only freed themselves and the slaves in both South Carolina and Florida, under the leadership command of "General Thomas Wentworth Higginson and Commander General David Hunter", headquartered in Hilton Head South Carolina in 1862. Even though President Abraham Lincoln rebuked it because he wasn't interested in freeing any slaves at that time, he was suggesting shipping all Negroes back to Africa.

Today-the year 2012 President Obama has won his second term in the White House, leaving not only a confused look on many white Americans faces, some appear to be down wright angry, where as in 2008 there was the look of great surprise. One week after the election twenty states begun to sign petitions to secede from the Union, which is unconstitutional, in 1861 South Carolina was the first State to secede from the Union, the exact same state who fired the first shot that started the Civil War! South Carolina is my home State, the State that I love, with the Confederate flag flying on the grounds in front of the State house. This flag represents a since of pride to the white South Carolinians', but to the African American and former descendants of slaves who made the same white descendants extremely wealthy and prideful, the flag is simply a beautiful sign of massive defeat for African Americans today, yesterday and all future days of the world's existence. You will see the thoughts and feelings of both the past and present and of both North and South in the following pages.

CHAPTER ONE

Just thinking

When I was just a small boy shortly after I started elementary school at age five, there was always the sincere question in my mind as I observed all of my surroundings in school, at my Church and in my community in general. On Saturdays we went downtown in Marion or Mullins, usually both on the same day where my Mom and Dad shopped, however the trip was mostly for us kids because we grew almost everything that we needed for food except sugar, tea and flour. Downtown I watched very vigilantly to try and locate a white man or woman who was larger in physical size than my Dad or any of the black men that I saw every day. I was terribly confused and I didn't want to ask anyone, what happened, or how in the world did these smaller white people wind up with all of this power over the black people as well as all of the money because the white people were the only ones who had both the money and power, and the black men were the strongest, largest and wisest in church.

Africa is the second largest continent on this planet, the United States can fit into Africa five Times, there are fifty two countries in Africa, Lake Victoria is the second largest and tallest waterfall in The world. Mount Kilimanjaro is the second highest mountain, second only to Mt. Everest.

In Africa, it is the black man who has the wright kind of hair; there are only three types of Hair that God created for all humanity, (1) Nappy hair for the black man because in Africa the daily Temperature ranges from one hundred and ten- to one hundred thirty degrees. Mud packs or protection on nappy hair in the sunshine. (2) Straight hair for whites and cooler climates for other races as Well. (3) curly hair-for white or black people in eastern parts of Africa, Ethiopia, Somalia, Egypt, Libya. The farther you go west in Africa the darker the skin color for protection from the sun, the farther that you go in Africa, the lighter –browner the skin color. Kings originated in Africa, however one King's territory might cover four to six countries and the king culture descends in that one family as King David, King Solomon etc. In our Holy Bible Genesis chapter (10) Noah had three sons who populated the earth after the flood. Shem-father of the oriental races and given the Asian continent. Ham (Black Ham whom Noah cursed his grandchildren for four hundred years in Egypt and God let it stand. (slavery). The sons of Ham are Cush, the oldest, name means Ethiopia, new name, Cush is the Hebrew word for Ethiopia. Mizraim, Hebrew word for Egypt, Phut, meaning Libya, and Canaan, founder of the Canaanites. Adam was given the seed of all nationalities and their genealogy. Africans ruled the world until the flood which was five thousand years. In 2011 the female Republican candidate Michelle Bachman said that African Americans were better off in slavery- it only took one hundred and forty six years for black people in America to rise from the worst form of degradation and suffering to the highest office in the land, President of the United States of America in 2008.

Ja'pheth, the youngest son of Noah, representing the white race and to fulfill the inherited curse of the enslavement of the grand children of Black Ham in Egypt for four hundred and thirty years. the Bible said that he who holds a people in bondage; he does it to his own hurt and that God himself would deal with him. Africans were taken from a land of total freedom, a land of riches and beauty. They were denied the wright to even speak their own languages, to date, African Americans are the only Race of any people to come to America or any other land and create their own knew language called "Gullah" spoken and practiced in Charleston South Carolina and have our own published Holy Bible.

Many years ago I read a great book written by Dr. Norman V. Peale which has propelled my thought process in varying directions, "The power of positive thinking", it opened my mind to new and fruitful enlightenment. I changed my mind about many things, the thought of America. The very same day that I was hired by Mutual of Omaha insurance company after resigning from the school district. You see I was given an oral prospectus test which was designed to determined my capability of the glass half empty, as far as taking chances to obtain a greater reward. The test was about wealth, as I was sitting there with my unit manager in his office, he just looked at me smiling for several minutes, so I politely asked, how badly did I fail? He didn't answer me he just said ED please, just hang on for one moment. He got up and rushed into his manager's office next door, the Division manager of the entire western part of South Carolina. I was dressed in a nice suit and tie, I looked myself over to see if I could determine what could possibly be wrong, was it something that I said to frighten this middle aged white man from Pittsburg. We were in the big beautiful gold glass building on Forest dr. and beltline streets, the fifth floor. I was the only black among thirty two white men and one white woman from North Augusta, however they were only about ten guys in the open bay area of the office and just myself and my new unit manager in his office. After about fifteen minutes they both came rushing in laughing and congratulating me for scoring so high on the test. The Division manager said that they had called the home office to check to find out if anyone had ever scored a 99 out of one hundred on this test, no one had, they said that they both were shocked; I had scored off of the charts in all areas, especially courage, the category that almost everyone fails, especially black candidates.

The one question that I missed read, ED how would you feel about having my name on a medicine bottle? It was an oral test and they're not allowed to advise or give you any help, I'd had Asthma as a child and grew out of it, which led me to think towards being sick, that's what medicine is for sick people. The other part of the dichotomy is the positive, the glass half full. The negative part is what I chose, no, I did not want my name on any medicine bottle, glass half empty, the glass being half full represents the ideology that if my name was on a medicine bottle, I would already be seriously rich because if that medicine is named after E. Graves that company and its distribution would all belong to me. They both wanted to take me out for cocktails but I said let's do it another day, rain check. I was pleased with my test score but I was highly saddened at never, never, never have I ever entertained such a lucrative thought. I said there's something that I must do right away and it can't wait. I walked right out of that office and took my note pad and drove over to BI-Lo, the grocery store on forest Dr. I walked down the first three isles and I was amazed at how many products on the shelves carried the names of so many business and white family names. I left the store and went directly to the library, it was time that I educate myself on the makers and shakers of America! I had just experienced an intellectual cunning and uplifting of the mind. My "awareness had heightened" Vitality, enthusiasm and an excitement came over me that I had never felt before and I never wanted to let that feeling go! Now, I wonder just how much other stuff have I been missing, I was thirty years old and never been on an airplane, never been out of the U.S. and I had only traveled or lived in four or five States just for summer jobs during college. It was all about to change, I would never think negatively ever again. from now on all of my thoughts would be positive, and there's always another way to get somewhere if the first effort fails.

I saw Johnson& Johnson products on the shelves, Swanson, Dove, Dial, I sold health insurance to Mr. and Mrs. J. Dial owners of dial soap. Milton" Hershey," Gortons, Stan back, Phillips, Campbell's, Hunts and Mr. Heinz. Welch's and great day, "Kellogg's" corn flakes. There was a colonel Kellogg in the Civil War in South Carolina Beaufort S.C. There was also a Libby's prison in Virginia during the Civil War. I found there to be absolutely so many white family names on the shelves of so many different stores that existed in both the American Revolution and Civil War until it is not funny! The only Black family names that I recognize now are Stubbs Barbeque and my classmate A. Johnson's husband's BBQ. Sauce in the Piggly Wiggly. I began to do some serious research on the study of Meta-physics, the Study of all human life forms. It was time that I educate myself over and beyond college curriculums. I needed to know all there was available to me concerning both Business development and the Philosophical thinking of the wisest and greatest minds that God sent into the world from long ago. this is the thing that I have committed the rest of my life to, learning new thinking processes and new ideas and philosophies of life that truly interest me. I have always loved studying new words and languages, it is extremely rewarding to me when I'm Reading and come upon a new and beautiful sounding word with a prolific meaning.

Many years ago I came upon a beautiful analogy of life that has completely changed my life. While studying the ideas of the great minds of Sages and pundits of the past, Men like Con Edison, Nicla Tesla, John D. Rockefeller, John Westinghouse, J.P. Morgan, Henry Ford, Walter Chrysler, John Du-Pont, Einstein, Aristotle, Plato, I came upon the geniuses who lived thirty five hundred to four thousand years before Jesus Christ was born. Great men like King Solomon, Diocletian, Roman Emperor, Thales, Phericides, Ptolemy, Vitruvius from Egypt. Patanjali from India, Permenides, Diogenes and finally my favorite, "Pythagoras from Greece;

Pythagoras was a great mathematician however in those days the brilliant minded students were assigned to the greatest teachers in the world, once the student had mastered all of the subjects that his teachers had to offer in their homeland, and Greece was renowned for great minds, they were allowed to travel to other lands of their own choosing for further studies. At age seventeen Pythagoras set sail for Egypt for three years. Upon returning home to Greece he began his quest to establish his own "Pythagorean school of thought. He took some of his students into the city square in Greece and begun to expound upon his philosophy of life. As they say, when the student is ready the teacher will appear. Pythagoras had a gathering of about three thousand people, most of whom were just peasants and farmers and had silent undivided attention as he begun. Life exist in spirit before the sperm enters the mother's womb. Once the male sperm makes the connection with the egg of the mother, God injects a part of his spirit at that moment and causes a fetus to become a living soul. The peasants and farmers didn't seem to get the idea completely so it just happens that the Zen master from India, Patanjili was visiting Greece and offered to give the young philosopher Pythagoras a helping hand in instruction. Patanjili was wearing an old smock type with large pockets and he just happened to have a few seeds left over from helping a farmer in his fields. He stepped up on the podium, took two watermelon seeds out of his pocket and held them up to the crowd and said comely, these are two simple watermelon seeds, if you take these and place them into a glass jar so that you will be able to see them every day, place a top with some holes punched in so that the seeds can receive air. Place the jar on your back porch or in a visible area so that you can see them clearly for one or two years, when the seeds begin to crack and break apart all that you have to do then is to place the broken seeds into the mother Earth that God has created, allow the seeds to be embraced by the warmth of the Sun and the rain, in days you will see that God has already placed inside the broken seeds, vines that will grow twenty to thirty feet long in all directions! Beautiful blossoms will appear which are too numerous to count, and everywhere there is a blossom a watermelon will come to grow and weight one hundred to two hundred times more than the seed that it came from. A human being can become broken and lost his or her way and suddenly realize that they can always go back to God and be made whole again, produce enormous fruit when they were once thinking of suicide!

The world created by God was made under the law of opposites and balanced on a wheel of order that exemplifies a high and a low, a warm and a cold, a wet and a dry, night and day, a sunset and a sunrise, so is life. Life is an intellectual experience of the mind. Pythagoras was the father of the word "Philosophy" but he had also been a student of Patanjili when he traveled to India, Rome, Egypt and other faraway lands during his wisdom seeking venture. The way that you think about things is key, having something exciting to look forward to is the key to living a happy life. That is the reason why I'm so saddened and disappointed that my high school class, the people who became my family in the first grade cannot convince themselves to answer a simple invitation to come and sit down and have a meal and share memories and thoughts with each other. There are seven stages of life, I'm 63 years old and in the senior stage until I reach age 76, although that might vary from person to person. Let me take this opportunity to read your mail to you, no one is competing with you anymore, and no one has any concerns about what kind of car that you drive and believe it or not absolutely no one cares anything about your house but you. Your house cannot help anyone but you. I've walked in and out of the homes of friends, family and clients in the insurance business and once I leave that home my feelings are always the same, that's a nice home, or that's a beautiful? and as I walked through I said nice pictures you have, that's a very nice back yard, actually I'm truly happy for you, but as soon as I leave your house; it is like flipping a light switch when I leave a room, forgotten. I am living currently in my third home and they all were nice but none were easy to pay for and my daughter's rooms were "shameful" and scary to enter. The IRS just took my second home. What has always discussed me is to see someone's face every day for years or every week for long periods of time and you walk up to greet that person at a function and they pretend that they don't know or have never known you. Let me hip you, just like you might not readily remember someone's name; make no mistake, there is always something about your spiritual presence that you remember. It leaves a very bad impression on folk when you think that you have done so well in life that you can't remember anything about someone that you have known all of your life. Happiness stays with you for short periods of time but sadness takes its own sweet time to leave you alone. Remember, we live in a world of opposites, joy and pain, Frankie Beverly-my kind of guy. No one cares who you married, I've been married for forty years to the same woman and when women over age fifty approach me with anything other than a smile or a hug, it is of no consequence or of interest to me. "Young women under fifty", there is nothing that I enjoy more than to see a beautiful woman, but I intend to absolutely enjoy spending and keeping my own money, I have children and grandchildren that I enjoy helping, but pretending that I don't. I truly am fascinated when I see a beautiful woman over seventy or eighty years old. My wife has more than enough of everything that I need and I had the opportunity to feel God's anger and displeasure with me in my younger years and I never want to experience that feeling ever again. Some white people strongly believe that a black man's greatest desire is to have a white woman, a red Cadillac, and a" gold tooth "neither has ever interested me in the least, I love a red avalanche and a yellow and black 1972 cutlass supreme.

Now, if you have ever truly been in love with someone, and that person has loved you back even if that person didn't love you equally, it is truly wonderful to have the opportunity to see that person on occasion it brings happiness too you, but, that is all that it is, just to see you or talk to you briefly. I miss talking to old girlfriends but that is all that it is! I miss you! No one has been given the power to choose the person that you fall in love with, particularly the first love, and that is always the love that God will not allow you to have. God is a God of perfect love and he only releases it to whom he will. The person that you are with right now will never tell you who their first love was, I did, I told my entire family and continue to do so because I find love to be so" independently fascinating," there's nothing equal to the power of love! If two people love each other equally, it will grow to be too great and God is a jealously God, he will not allow it. After I read the" power of positive thinking" by Dr. Norman Vincent Peale and found that he actually grew up knowing Henry Ford, D. Cadillac and Walter Chrysler and others of that era that attended his Church occasionally, having something to always look forward to, failure becomes an illusion, they are simply obstacles, road blocks that you are supposed to find your way around, you simply used the wrong approach, think about it and try it another way. There are different realms and degrees of love, as there are different realms in God's Kingdom. Love is the only thing that I cannot get around or out of, so I decided long ago that I would simply embrace it, it gives me peace and pleasure.

Black men and women have nappy hair, a word that sounds distasteful or disgraceful, I used to cut hair when I was in high school to keep money in my pockets. I grew up on a large farm and we always ate very good, smothered steak or smothered chicken, grits that we grinded out of our corn and hot biscuits for breakfast. Sunday dinner was always a great feast with two kinds of meat, fried chicken roast beef, fried chicken and ham, fried chicken pork chops, and although I don't eat much pork now I cannot and do not want to get away from fried chicken. We worked all of the time and there was no money to be had. Black women can braid their hair many different styles, curl or straighten it, they can naturally wear it in a bush, no other ethnicity has that option. Seven braided dread locks were cut from Samson's head and many people in Gaza still wear their hair in braids today. Having the experience of cutting hair I found curly hair to be the most difficult. Having said that, I found it rather easy to find my barber when I went to college, my friend and barber, Grip. Opps, I almost forget to conclude my idea of preference; black women come in all colors, adequate choices for the black man. Even though I'm aware of the fact that the skin of fried chicken is harmful to your moderation is the key and it will take some work for me yet to back off.

CHAPTER TWO

Happy Feelings

I was a very happy kid growing up in Rains, my hometown. Excitement was always nearby, there were ten or twelve cows, three big and powerful mules, several hogs, chickens, ducks, geese, every animal that you can think of, we had it, except sheep, no sheep. There was always something fun for me to do because I was always hiding in the woods with our dog brownie; When I heard my name called I just pretended that I didn't hear it unless it was meal time, I knew that any other time was a call to do some work! Many days after my friend Lee and I finished selling our soda bottles that we picked up along 501highway which ran right down through Rains, or selling the eggs that we stole from our farm. There were eggs in hay stacks, in tall grass, in the edge of the woods under pine trees in the pine straw and at Easter time I never found not one boiled egg at school, I walked right past eggs in the grass that I looked under and someone would come right behind me and pick up eggs and laugh at me.

Lee and I would sit on a tree ranch in the edge of the woods watching the new and beautiful cars going by both winter and during summer months there was a continuous flow of traffic. While we ate our huge baby Ruth candy bars which cost ten cents as did ice cream sandwiches we played a game of selecting the prettiest cars that we claimed were ours. I always chose Chevrolets and Buicks while Lee favored Fords and Mercury's. I never said anything to Lee but it saddened me that we only saw white people driving those cars, never any blacks, Orientals or Mexicans, now why is that. The cars had license plates from every State in the Union but none of the cars had black families or occupants. I had already made my mind up the year before when I was four; I was without any doubt going to be a rich businessman, all I had was to wait on time. Back to the Easter egg hunt, my first in the spring of 1954 first grade. My little brother DG had been asking every day to take him to school with me. DG woke me up early that Thursday morning to the smell of hot biscuits and smothered chicken, grits and eggs. My older brothers and sisters were laughing and talking about the high school where they went on the bus after walking with us. As soon as we got up from the table I realized that DG didn't eat much of anything. He had his new blue jeans and new brogan shoes on and was too excited to eat! We stepped outside and mom gave us a hug and waved goodbye. As we begun to walk I noticed the color of the ground was grayish from the dew. Birds were chirping as they did every morning and as we walked past the cow pasture the cows just walked over and stared at us. DG started tugging on my shirt sleeve as it was warm in early spring with flowers and the smell of honeysuckle was very prevalent. I said what is it DG, Abalie (Arvanie) my middle name that he couldn't pronounce correctly yet he was four and I was six. What all did Mom put in our lunch bag? I said I don't know maybe we should take a quick look;

I opened the lunch brown paper bag first and saw wrapped in wax lunch wrapping paper four warm absolutely great aromatic fragrance smell of two grape jelly biscuits and two butter biscuits, wow! I said gaa-ait day! Then I opened my lunch bucket and there was two beautiful fried chicken Sandwiches. Boy oh boy,

I closed the box back up real quick before DG could see clearly. He said what else do we have in the lunch box, I said chicken sandwiches, our eyes met and we both laughed yum yum. Now, we had about a mile and a half or two mile walk and my older brothers always walked much faster than I did, they had to catch the bus to Centenary, Terrill's bay high which was six miles away. DG begun to work on me, he said Abalie, let's just taste one of the biscuits? I said no, we have to eat at recess on the playground after the Easter egg hunt, what time is that going to be he said? Eleven thirty. There was another yank on my sleeve only a couple of moments later, can we just taste one biscuit he said? I said it's not going to be very long at all you'll see. Abalie, let's just taste one of my biscuits, together, I looked down at him and remembered that he had not finished his breakfast and I knew that he was hungry so I opened the bag and took out a butter biscuit, broke it and gave him half. Now what in the world did I do that for? He and I continued to walk and taste the residual effect of that biscuit. Before he yanked on my shirt sleeve again I looked down at him and he was smiling up at me with his lips closed as I had never seen him do before in his life. I said let's try one more time, a jelly biscuit this time, ok, ok. We ate the jelly biscuit and that was all she wrote, DG knew that I couldn't stop once I got the flavor of the warm jelly biscuit in my mouth that's the way it always is with everyone in our family, it doesn't have to be a lays potato chip, you can't eat just one. By the time we got to the school grounds we didn't even have a bag any more, we had two chicken sandwiches in the lunch bucket, I looked down at my brother licking his lips, took the lunch box, put it under my arm and ran to the school door. 501 highway has always been busy, Rains is only 37 miles from

15

myrtle Beach and that's the big attraction. Atlantic Beach, the Black Beach is 10 miles further South on 501. Today it is almost non-existent. Time brings along with it many changes in the way that we look and feel about many things.

Typical Day On College Campus

During the school year of 1969 and 1970 there was a young man from Spartanburg that we called "MAC", A handsome young man whom I observed as polite and mature minded. He came to school with owning his own car, a beautiful black 1964 Chevy super sport and the look of a true Businessman. He was dating a cute sweetheart whom we will call "Lacie" a tall dark good-looking girl who also had the look of a confident successful Business woman as well. I'm proud to say that my predictions were correct in both cases however I was both proud and surprised that she made a career change early in life just as I did however she chose to except a position at S.L.E.D., The prestigious State Law Enforcement Division- She became a private investigator with earned high security clearance, (Lacie).

I always had trouble getting my tuition bill caught up after The Dean at Morris College abused my work ethics and absconded with my work study checks. Many times I had to go to the Business manager of the College to get him to write a note to the Dietician in the cafeteria to allow me to eat for a few days until I could raise the money to pay my bill.

I left school for a year in 1970 to work and to volunteer the draft into the US. Navy to avoid being drafted into the Army and go straight to Vietnam. When I returned in the fall of the following year my class had graduated and there was a female student body president handing out flyers and conducting meetings with the express idea of simply boycotting the cafeteria in order to force the cooking staff to prepare better meals in the cafeteria and to build a new girls dorm. The Night before the boycott was to begin the following morning at breakfast I decided to go to the meeting just to see who the young lady was yielding this great power over everyone and no one was challenging her motives and tactics. I stood up and asked her how long she was intending to stick to her guns with this big idea, and how was the entire student body of over 600 students going to eat for the indefinite period of time, she said boldly and proudly, I can feed the entire campus if necessary. I said these students have already paid for those and no one is going to re-reimburse us for the meals that we miss and the President will simply tell the cafeteria staff to refrigerate the one meal until we break down, that's exactly what I would do, and walked out of the meeting. The next morning my two younger homeboys came by my room and asked me what was I going to do. I said" boys' this is the first year that I've been able to pay my tuition bill on time and I'll be dog gone if I 'm going to follow this little dumb girl who has a few dollars in her pocket, It's not going to do us one bit of good when we get stomach pains all day and all night. Get your coats! But Graves, the entire campus is outside the caféteria door just waiting with signs for us, we heard some other boys talking about you last night, they're not going to let us in. I said have you ever seen or heard of anyone beating or stopping Arvanie Graves, no, without hesitation, well let's get it on! I walked out of the dorm doors across the campus with my two young sidekicks whom I used feed Chica-dee Chicken with my gambling money that I won playing tunk every week. Everyone stood way back and just watched as we went into the dining hall and took our time enjoying a wonderful breakfast. The cooks laid out a special meal for us that morning with three different types of sausages, scrambled eggs with cheese and all the fixings. That went on for three days until lunch time that Friday about fifty boys in my dorm ask if I would come and talk to them- a committee of the female followers. I went in and the student body Vice president ask me, why was I deliberately breaking the boycott strike, that's the reason we as students can't ever get anything done. I said young man, just two years ago James Brown made a record" called" it's a man's world, and in the garden of Eden God made Adam out of the earth as he did all of the other animals, but he never went back into the Earth to make anything else, God made Eve out of Adam's rib and he made woman for the man and he gave the laws of the universe to Adam to be the head of the household and family. Adam however listened to his wife, made a foolish mistake, when she tasted the fruit nothing happened, but when she convinced Adam to break God's law, the whole world changed, the countenance of his glorified body fell, and because you know that it is impossible for students to win a poor unthought-of plan such as voluntarily missing meals that your parents struggled to pay for all of you and no one is going to re-reimburse you for the great meals that you all have already missed. Every day, I saw pretty young girls walking out in front of the dining hall starring in with heads bowed like little puppies. One of the boys said "that's it", ED Graves is right I'm with Graves, and so the strike ended and everything went back to normal except the same thing that always happened, the female president got kicked out of school.

That afternoon after classes were over I was asked to come back to the student lounge to lecture some more about responsible manhood, the Bible's version.

It was the school year of 1970-71, I went into the Dobbins-Keith dormitory where we lived and there was a gathering of about fifty or so young men waiting, I was a year or two older than most men present. I began as I had often done in my Sunday class. Let us go back to Man's beginning, in "Africa", the place where all of the creations of animals live. In the Bible book of Genesis, it clearly states that God told his highest serving Angels-let us make man to "Replenish—Replenish the Earth, meaning that the earth has been habitated many times before but they didn't work out as God planned using their free will. I used to be totally dissatisfied with the way that the white man took the land of America from the Indians, however our Bible shows time and time again that when the people who are thriving in a land or not that God gave them, he took the land by empowering other tribes to defeat and subdue that land for themselves. The Indians didn't do anything with this beautiful land of America didn't even build a toilet, just dug a hole and moved on with their other Gods. After God made Adam from the earth he was alone, without woman, he told Adam to subdue the land- make it his own and name every tree and every animal. After Adam named all of the animals which probably took one hundred years, God took a walk in the cool of the evening along the sea shore as he did every day, teaching and imparting wisdom to him because God is the only place where you get wisdom, old age and gray hair gives you experience only, what to do and what not to do, and no one is able to adequately use wisdom until they reach thirty years of age as Jesus was when he started his ministry. Adam asked God, why is all of the male animals prettier" and more beautiful than the females? The Lion is bigger with a powerful body and main about his head, weighing five hundred and fifty, the female weights three hundred and fifty pounds. The Bull is big ferocious and powerful whereas the cow looks meek with an utter for suckling. The blue jay and the Robin, red birds and the like are all larger with more lavish feathers, the Stallion, most beautiful of all is the male horse.

God told Adam that he has made all of the males for his glory and I 'm going to make woman for man's glory but beware, the woman's glory is always going to be her hair. Woman has been given an intrinsic intuition that is unmatched. She will give birth to all of the children of the earth, but it is you Adam who will possess the seed and geologies of all the races on earth. The woman shall be under your protection and care, you must love and cherish her, and ultimately, you must be willing to risk your life to protect her. If you allow the woman to lead you and make important decisions above your knowledge, it will cause an imbalance in the laws of nature and the universe over time that I have established from the foundations of the world. She will be a helper to you, meaning that if she sees and realizes that you are going about something the wrong way or there's a better way to do something, let the woman come to you with the suggestion, don't you think that it would work better if you do it this way, you will be making the final decision even if she has tricked you into thinking that it was your idea from the beginning. For that reason, the woman was made for the man Adam, she is the only creation that God has made to be more "beautiful" than the males of all other animals on earth! She is the only creation that God did not make from the earth.

While Adam was at work tending his garden which was projected to be about 25,000 acres the wise and tremendously handsome Lucifer-(Satan) was romancing Eve, Adam's wife. He beguiled her, there are Biblical historians who send me research information for ON TTRACC Bible-Business College of which I'm the founder, information from The University of Jerusalem and many other Colleges around the world. Some information suggest that Satan had assumed the body of a man, beautiful, most handsome of all Angels in Heaven and he romanced Eve and convinced her to taste the fruit of the tree of good and evil. Nothing happened when Eve eat of the fruit but when she led Adam and convinced him to eat of the fruit, the axis of the foundation of the earth trembled and began to erupt into great and tremendous earth quakes, all of the animals that Adam could call and they came to him humbly, started to fear him and ran from him. No vegetables would grow freely and bountifully as before, weeds and grass began to take over Adam's garden and he had to develop different kinds of fertilizer to get his vegetables to grow and produce. The four rivers that had flowed through the Garden of Eden bring- new life and various kinds of fish for food—two of the rivers diverted, stopped flowing through the garden. Adam and Eve were kicked out simply because Adam did not stand up and take his place and authority. Eve was his wife he was supposed to take her into conference, not hit her, and as long as he remained under God's authority and kept Eve under his authority as God told him, the world would still be perfect; That was in the year 1971, what I say to students and others now has additions.

God took Adam's land just as he has done throughout the Old Testament of our Holy Bible. From Genesis to Malachi which is comprised of only Black and Brown people, as I said earlier the father east you travel in the African Continent the lighter the skin color is but those people are all Africans, which means that king David was not a red headed white King, neither was Solomon, Goliath, Samson and all other characters in the Old Testament, we encountered the Caucasian white race in the New Testament, Rome, Mathew, Mark, Luke and John. In the early 1990's I began to recognize the transitional change that was taking place in America and the world at large. South Africa, the most segregated place on Earth elected a Black President, Mandela. In two thousand eight America elected its first black President also, Barack Obama, the son of a Black South African man Obama's farther, andin 2012 President Obama was reelected for his second term. Sadam Husain, Osama Benlaudin, Kaddafi and others have been dethroned or killed, It is said by wise men of the past history that every new millennium, God causes the land and wealth to change hands, I make no mistakes about God's world he made the whole world and created everything that is in the world and he can do anything that he wishes because he is in total control and we cannot see him and even if we could there would still be nothing anyone could do but observe.

Then and Now

To continue, when God said that man should not be alone, he took Adam for a long walk along the see shore to teach him the difference between "Wisdom and Knowledge" for three days.

He told Adam to look at the vastness of the Sea and not only is this the only one, there are seven Seas representing the number of completion. He told Adam to look down into the water, there were two trails of sea creatures that were too small to see with the naked eye. As God and Adam continued to walk the fish got larger in shapes and sizes until in the cool of the evening of the third day, there were two great blue whales, the Bylenne is the largest of the whale family which consist of forty different species of whales. The blue great whale grows in length sixty to one hundred and ten feet long, "dat's" longer than a basketball court. He weights from eighty to two hundred and ten tons. Ton (2000) pounds. The great whale eats well over twelve thousand pounds of seafood per day and guest what? what ED? The great blue whale does not have any teeth he doesn't need teeth, just like when we eat our meals they continue to cook at 98.6 degrees for two hours until the food is digested, the whale just go for a four or five hundred mile swim and cook his fish, he prefers squid. Now Adam, that is knowledge. He told Adam that at various places in the Oceans the bottom comes to the top, we call it the tide comes in. The Ocean can take your life at a moment's notice, but look out over the deep and see forty and fifty foot waves standing. If one single drop of this water were to be cast too far inland and gets separated from the ocean body out onto the sea shore(sand) that single drop of water knows to go through the sand down to the water table and be gathered back into the ocean where it came from-back to its God. So no matter how far you go away from me, or how broken and torn that you get, you can always come back to me, your God, that is Wisdom. God placed a mini version of both heaven and earth inside Adam's heart during creation in the spirit world, invisible to the naked eye. Anytime that we look into our hearts as in meditation, we can see our love ones and our dreams and purposes. It is time now to take hold of your dream that you laid aside years ago for various reasons. (Ancient historians tend to always decide that when they come upon or discover knowledge of the evidence of magnificent accomplishments in the world where it is determined that the inhabitants of that era were of Black skin color, they come to the conclusion that the people had to have been of any other nationality than the black race. In Egypt pure black people ruled during the building of the great Pyramids from the thirteenth to the twenty fifth dynasty, and then the ruler ship went back to brown skin color. Iraq has been picked to be where the garden of Eden was but in 1986 or 1987 Time magazine printed on the cover of its magazine a picture of a black Adam and Eve accompanied by the findings of Adams bones in "Kenya" with Eve's bones in a cave ten miles away. I kept the magazine cover and framed it, it's on my office wall in my home.

In the 1990's I saw with my own eyes, OJ Simpson walk out of jail first, then out of the court house a free man after being arrested and charged with double murder of a white woman and a white man in California. In the 1960's men were picked up on public drunk charges and hanged in jail with both hands cuffed behind their backs and the news media reported that they all hung themselves, in Rains and all over this Country. I saw with my own eyes on TV for several weeks, a black lawyer, Johnny Cochran clears OJ Simpson of all charges against a team of white and a black lawyer of double murder of the two white people and I know Italians in Baltimore who told me that OJ never killed anyone. My advice would have been to tell OJ Simpson to leave the Country for at least ten years but I know that OJ thought that the white people loved him. In the 1990's I saw on national TV, a black man named Richard Williams with no teeth, raise and teach his two youngest daughters Venus and Serna Williams to be the coveted title holders of both Wimbledon and the US Open Tennis Championships and were the number one and number two in the world for several years. In 2011 and 2012 I saw a black male swimmer take the bronze medal in the Olympics, and in 2012 I saw Gabriel Gifford win the Gold medal in gymnastics, first in history of the Olympics. I have two daughters whom I raised and could never get them to even clean their rooms. No parent has ever raised one of their children to become champions as Richard Williams has so who am I are anyone else to say anything about his teeth!

When men allow their wives to lead them the wives wind up on basketball wives and the husbands wind up broke. Tiger was wrong so he paid just like Mike but these guys are not broke. There will be no such thing as the South will rise again the world is in transition and nothing will ever go back to where it was, if the Confederates had won the Civil War they would have surely had it made but God said that it was time, Time for the bottom to come to the top. As the black race, we are not hardly interested in retaliation on the whites, the one thing that sustained us through the horrors of slavery was the powerful belief that one day God would take us out of bondage and our children would go into God's wealthy place. We have always known what God does to those who hold another people in bondage. In 1961 Ingarmar Johanson, a white German boxer defeated the heavy weight Champion of the world Floyd Patterson, six months later Floyd Patterson beat I. Johanson and took his title back and the rest is history, there hasn't been another white heavy weight boxing champion of the world since and none in sight.

In 1961 a white man from West Columbia opened and started the BI-LO grocery store food chain stores. He died in 1966 and his children sold the stores to a sweetish company and in 2004 it was sold again to a company called Atold from Sweden also. A family from Charleston founded the Piggy Wiggly stores, there are Mexican grocery stores in Charlotte and all over the US. There are no known grocery stores in South Carolina owned by blacks.

CHAPTER THREE

Civil War From The
Black Hand Side

Before we get into the inner workings and the mind of the Slave vs. the mind of the white slave masters, I would like to invite you to take a trip with me back in time to see just who it was that the slave traders brought out of Africa! We know that Africa was the cradle of civilization, there is only two rivers flowing through Iraq and there are no Lions, tigers, bears and wilder beast in Iraq. Before God placed Adam in the Garden of Eden he placed Gold, onyx and many other valuable diamonds, oil silver, uranium, none of which has ever left the Earth, lots and lots though have left Africa. Man was never meant to be poor and broke.

From Adam to the flood was two thousand two hundred and twelve years time. From the flood to Abraham was nine hundred and twelve years, (912). From Abraham to Moses was four hundred and thirty years (430) it was Abraham who God told that everywhere that his foot treed, he was going to give him the land. It is the African slave whose feet have treed over America, Europe Spain Portugal all of the Islands and many other Countries, some I know of and some I don't. From Moses to David five hundred and ten years (510), from David to Babylon (old name for Iraq), five hundred years (500) from the Babylonian captivity to the incarnation of Jesus Christ was four hundred years (400) for a total of five thousand, five hundred (5,500) years. Africans ruled the world for the first five thousand years, there was no America at that time. It took the Indians five hundred plus years to walk-migrate to the land that we call America. Adam was not supposed to ever die he was supposed to live until Jesus came and go back with him. That is why it is written in our Bible that when Jesus gave up the ghost on the cross, they saw dead men walking! There is no sure way for archeologist to determine how old the Earth- world is, but man has been on the earth for a little over seven thousand (7,000) years. God's world has always been, same as he is, you get it, his name is I am that I am! He is everywhere all of the time, there is no carnal way to understand that. The Hittites were the most feared and most powerful African tribe in existence for many years they defeated Egypt, the brown people, descendants of Noah's son, black ham's second son whose name was Egypt! The Hittites were in Jericho when the walls came tumbling down and today in both Jericho and "Aswan" southern Egypt the people are blue black! For a long time the Masai tribe lived in the mountains of Kenya where the average height was seven feet tall for men and six foot five to six foot seven for the woman, where Eve's bones were found.

In a book called "They came before Columbus" Africans came by ship and traded with the Indians long before Columbus or any other Europeans for centuries. They brought collard plants, turnips, mustards, watermelons, cantaloupes, so of course black people love watermelons. Okra and butter beans and peas came from Africa.

In the year 1526 historical documents were found to contain evidence of the slave trade but 1619 at Jamestown Virginia is our most noted deliverance of the African slave. They were indentured slaves, meaning that after working for seven years they were free however those slaves chose to work a few more years to earn enough money to travel back to Charleston South Carolina where seventy five to eighty percent of the slaves were being delivered at that time. From the time the slaves arrived in Jamestown Virginia until they reached Charleston SC. there was absolutely no need for a police force in America but as soon as the free blacks arrived in Charleston which was 1641, they formed a police force in Charleston SC. FOR BLACK PEOPLE! In 1660 the Pinker tons were formed for the purpose of spying on rich aristocratic white people. In 1672 the King of England formed the Royal African Company for the transportation of African slaves, "Black Gold". In 1860 a young eighteen year old slave was worth two thousand five hundred dollars, was like having a top of the line brand new Cadillac, except the slave could not only reproduce several children, twenty to forty with two or three different women, he worked in the Massa's f fields and could be hired out to earn money for Massa on Saturday and Sundays, by the end of the seventh century twice as many black slaves were in America as whites. The Pinker tons evolved into the FBI, Federal Bureau of Investigations today.

In 1792 Eli Whitney graduated from Yale University and took a trip to Savanna Georgia, which borders South Carolina and took a position as a tutor in a Revolutionary War General's home, he saw slaves using a contraption which separated seeds from cotton. Eli Whitney borrowed the money for a patent application and the cotton Gin was born. As all inventions are born out of need to ease the pain of work. Only poor white people worked, an as soon as they raised the money to purchase one slave, quit working. In eighteen sixty the slaves were worth more than all of the Banks, all of the stock, all of the automobiles, all of the financial institutions in America put together, the Northern States had evolved and became industrialized and did not need slaves anymore verses the whites in the South who were continuously transporting slaves and getting richer and not working themselves at all, not even taking out their own pea pots, so guest what? What ED? You Know I'm glad that you asked me. They said "Thar's got to be a war "South Carolina said you must be crazy, and immediately became the first State to succeed from the Union. (Foot note, World book encyclopedia.)

Now, let's take a look and see just who the whites went to the great big Africa, five times larger than America and got to work for them forever for free. The white man could not hide in Africa, everything was black owned and operated, the airports are owned in Africa today. The whites hired blacks to capture the African slaves—God said that he was going to cripple the right arm of the blacks because we became arrogant and chose to always- got to have some other kind of God that they could make or capture and place them in their homes and places of worship. It is difficult to learn how to think like God as the wise men say, God allowed the white man to take the most powerful, most resilient and some of the most intelligent people on Earth to be captured, enslaved for four hundred years twice. Our bodies are going to die but our spirits will live forever in other bodies but your minds memories will be wiped clean. God kept saying to the children of Israel, I am your God who brought you out of Egypt long after those generations had died out, same spirit different bodies. The slave traders brought out of Africa Jack Johnson, Joe Louis, Muhammad Ali and all of the skilled and powerful minded people to America and after one hundred and forty six years the bottom has come to the top. No other people in History in any country has ever risen from slavery to the highest post of power in the world. The slave has always known that it was God who allowed him to be enslaved and the only thing for the slave to do was survive-live until God said its time! The first few years the slaves were truly victims, they were not allowed to congregate at all. A slave ship would pick up its cargo of for instance a family of eight among the load and travel to Brazil, trade two family members for spices and such, on to Portugal and sell two for tobacco, on to the Virgin Islands, Jamaica etc. for sugar from the sugar cane fields and sell one to England, drop off several to include one from that family to pay for the financing of the trip. By that time there's only one or two left out of the family of eight who left Africa together never to see each other again. So when the slaves arrive in Charleston SC. and sold to various plantation owners to be distributed throughout this State and others, they went through a grieving process. They had to learn a second language which he or she is ridiculed horribly and called dumb lazy nigger. Christopher Columbus was a slave trader. The slave has to learn how to take hollering and yelling from sun up until sundown and beaten if they don't catch on fast enough. They are fed meager meals with insufficient vitamins which causes the first generation of slaves growth to be stunted for forty years. The mentality of the slave owner was to steal-um breed-um work-um until they are old and useless, many died young from tremendous laborious activity. The slave had no childhood, as soon as they could walk they were put to work. Feed them as cheaply as possible. But the slave quickly learn their roll and adapt. My grandfather, My Dad and my uncles told me many, many stories and I asked all of the right questions to get them in the mood to tell me.

The slave always knew what the whites were thinking but the whites never knew what the blacks were thinking. My Granddad said that he could tell whether a white was good or bad from a hundred feet away, he said that they carried their hatred in their spirit and he could feel it from a long ways off. It is just like the feeling that you get when someone is starring angrily from behind you. When the slave master heard the slaves singing or dancing they thought they were happy, when instead they were diverting the Massa's attention while the slick Robert lee and Jessie Lee were stealing and ringing the necks of two chickens they stole from mass's chicken coop for the family supper that night.

When I was young, eight or ten years old my Dad would hire me and my brothers out to work on the white man's farm to earn money which we never got any of. Working in tobacco and cotton fields but mostly tobacco because I was not going to let on to just how much cotton that I could pick. Forty five pounds was the most and then I laid down on my sack under the tall cotton after I let everyone leave me behind. Cotton was back breaking work and I didn't care how much I was teased because some little children would past right by me and pick over one hundred pounds, six and seven years old girls and boys, didn't bother me in the least, you see if you picked one hundred pounds today guess? Tomorrow they want you to pick one hundred and fifty pounds. In the tobacco fields cropping tobacco you could work at your own pace, although you're still bending and hurting your back. It started out this way, my four older brothers and I along with the farmer's special hired hand, "the slave driver". He was paid a dollar extra but always an older guy who taught you the ropes as soon as the farmer left the scene to go to the barn or go drink Pepsi's and crackers and tell jokes and talk about us at the local convenience store. "Awe right boys let's git it". As soon as the farmer left, take your time, and when you got to the end of the row, "take a break now". You see the farmer has several fields of tobacco and as soon as you finished one he took you to the next, a method has to be established, if the man has five acres of tobacco and five croppers, we're only going to finish two fields today and save two for the next day, he's only paying you six dollars per day to stay in the hot sun ninety plus degrees and if it rains, let's git it boys! That's how it was passed down to us from slavery, if you allow the slave owner to work you to death, to him it would be just like flipping a light switch when you leave a vacant room. To the slave owner the slave was just like his hogs, breed um and eat um and breed the slave and sell um. The slave was created just to make the white man rich and ninety eight percent of America's wealth is a result of slavery. In the 1800's John DuPont invented gun powder with the wealth his family received from slave labor. The slave was thought of as inhuman, couldn't care for himself and needed to always have someone white to watch over them. The poor whites could feel important by whipping anyone's slave and take him or her to the master and say that he captured your property for you, and get a couple of bucks to boot for stopping a runaway slave. New York life insurance company was the first to underwrite an insurance policy for a runaway slave$500.00. The slave was working in the north field all along.

In 1861 William C. Durant, called Billy Crapo was born to Henry Howland Crapo, wealth from slavery allowed Billy Durant to found General Motors in Flint Michigan, also AC-Delco. Louis Chevrolet was a mechanic for Henry Ford and a race car driver before he built the Chevrolet. Henry Ford worked on his Dad's farm and as an apprentice engineer for Con Edison.

Bank of America was founded as Bank of Italy in 1904 by Amadeo Peter Giannini in Italy. In 1998 it became Nations Bank and has since evolved into the largest bank in America. Wells Fargo was founded by Henry Wells and William Fargo in 1852, started as stage coaches. Slavery topped everything. In South Carolina the public Libraries are loaded with shelves of books on the Civil War. I enjoy my history channels, I have four and I can always find footage and documentaries on the Civil War, it is November 2012 and the movie "LINCOLN" was just released. Half of the streets in our Cities are Named after Civil War Generals. I am not angry at the whites for loving their History, I love my history too, your history is just like your home town, no one loves it like you do. I enjoy watching the John Wayne Civil War movies and I understand why they didn't include the brave and cunning acts that the slaves were successful in. They were excellent spies for the Union and if Lincoln had not sent in the black soldiers, the union would have certainly lost the war. The slaves knew before the Southern Whites that the Union Soldiers were coming and they started running to the east and running to the west and running weather the Union loved them the best or not. The white slave owners didn't have a clue they thought that their slaves were happy and didn't have since enough to know any better. "Naaw" my slaves love me and my family to death, they wouldn't leave me if I gave um de money and two ah my best mules to go wid, didn't have a clue!

Every city in America and all other prominent Countries have designed their Cities after Rome. As soon as you get into the out skirts of Charlotte North Carolina traveling on I-77 interstate there is street sign that reads "Tyvola" a major city in Rome. Charlotte is the capital of NC. and the home of the major Banks to include "Bank of America". Any City in any State in America you will find that the tallest building in the City is owned by an insurance company, and that company leases the first floor to a major bank. As soon as you walk over to the elevators you will see the wall calendar has a listing of all the insurance products upstairs on every floor. In Marion South Carolina my home town has an abundance of streets named after the "Swamp Fox" officers in the American Revolutionary War.

Super Star Slave Actors-Actresses

On a slave plantation every man woman and child knew exactly where the slave master was at all times. A child was taught beginning at the age of three, how to draw a circle in their minds around the entire property, until you get to the entrance gate or the cross roads bordering the land. Once the word was passed that Mass'a was gone to town, the hoes dropped where they were. There was a hog or two killed and butchered, chickens were killed and plucked in the woods and feathers and hog hair and blood buried quickly. The mules being plowed in the fields, woe mule at the end of the row, take a break. The slaves learned very early on that when you started to working for Massa as soon as the slave driver left, you slow the mule and all work down. If you let on to how much you could do, whatever it was that you did yesterday you were expected to do much more today. The slaves developed a method, work as slow as you can when the slave driver is away and as soon as you were alerted by a slave song or whistle, speed up and look lively. The slaves learned three or four different facial expressions when they were in the presence of the boss. You knew when to show extreme fear, extreme sorrow when someone in mass's family were sick or died. Extreme pain when you wanted to get out of work, and extreme humility when you wanted something from the boss, like borrow a 410- or 22 rifle to go hunting for game at night after work and you always hid the best game behind the barn before you went and gave Massa a rabbit. Anytime that he showed up, everyone knew just how to step and fetch it. You knew how to pretend to be as dumb as a box of broken rocks sitting on the back porch, waay back in the woods, of an abandoned house. There was always a black preacher or someone who learned to read and taught a select few. The slave knew every inch of massa's property woods and all.

The slave traders brought the great Wilma Rudolph's, the Arthur Ashe's Venus and Serena's out of Africa. They brought the Great Jim Brown's, OJ. Simpsons, Barry Sanders and all of the great heavy weight champions out of Africa and thought they could always keep and past down there inherited Slave wealth, Wilt Chamberlain, Bill Russell, Kareem and Mike. If there was an adjoining plantation that had roaming cows, hogs geese, chickens, they got stolen without enough to be noticed. The Republican candidate Michelle Bachman's Grandparents and parents past down that same dumb idea that they treated their slaves well so naturally they and many others thought that the slave would be better off working for them for free, being sold off from their families. We are the only people who have family members sprinkled all over the world during the slave trade, even Russia. Once I was having lunch with a young dumb white guy when I was in the insurance business and leading the entire sales force in sales from our branch office, the guy said right out of the blue Ed, I know that you wish that you were white, we did ya-ll a big favor when we brought you out of Africa, you could have been eaten! I just looked at him for a good while. you mean to have one color hair, a different color mustache and different color eyes. I can brush my hair and it will wave, what can your hair do. Do you mean that I want to have white skin that is not white, belong to a race of people who slaughtered old men women and children while they slept, the Indians, how long do you think that they will hate you without you knowing it. It was your race who dropped the Atom bomb on the Japanese, old men women and children, do you think that they will ever forget you? Your color is right in America right now but this is God's country and one day you will not be on top and right in this Country. We left the restaurant and changed and went on the tennis court and I beat him three sets, 6-0, 6-0,6-0. He wasn't satisfied, well let's go inside a play some ping pong, he didn't have a clue, I beat him 11-0 a skunk three consecutive times before he could even get a single point. I served him five different serves five times in a row before he ever got one point. He said ED, you told us that the word Nigger was not offensive to you right, I said nope, I hope the word cracker is not offensive to you. he said no, I said there's no word in the English language that's offensive to whites because you're the majority power here and everything in America is made and owned by you, you could care less what I call you. He said that's right but I never thought of it quite that way. But you are the "baddest nigger that any of us have ever seen, we ain't never seen a black person that could do everything good, and on top of that we all said that we ain't never seen a black person who could swim, and beat us at that too; The first day that I introduced myself to the sales team in the Mutual of Omaha office, being the only black among thirty two whites, Gentleman and one lady, My name is ED Graves, there is no reason for you to become uncomfortable around me when you use the word "black," and Nigger is an ignorant person regardless of what color they are. However I believe that if we get rid of the word entirely, less than one hundred years from now, our black history will be stolen again. Martin Luther King Jr. will wind up white in all of our History books, just like all of the Bible characters are white along with Jesus. Don't tell me that you believe that our sweet Jesus is "black" I said just look at where he came from the east, there was no America back then just Europe, Rome-new testament. The names of the most powerful warrior tribe in the Bible were the Hittites whose name were changed to the physicians in our ancient history books. White America did not want anyone to know that medicine and mathematics was discovered by the black African. When I left this cat I began to do some serious thinking about what the whites are thinking about when they see a black person. I went into my back yard and lit my charcoal grill and had a few cocktails, thinking. The mortgage on my home was owned by Bank of America, I had three cars only one was paid for, my cutlass, the other two was stilled owned by my credit union, white people. I remembered each time that I went to the home office in Omaha Nebraska the only black people I saw were just a few in the building that had come from other States for the sales training schools. The pilot was white, the President of both Mutual and United of Omaha companies were white. In the early 1980's all of the Bank branch managers and tellers were white. The Governor and Mayer were white and as I began to notice all grocery store managers were white. So I understood the white guy from my office who thought that all black people wanted to be white. Well that's a seriously bad mistake, I've always known that I was the Grandson of a King, knowing in your heart that you are a King and there is nothing or no one between you and God who made Adam in his image in Black Africa, I've always known that the world was my playground; it was just a matter of finding my place in the world. Ha ha I started to laugh really hard in my back yard; here it was all over again just like it was when I was a kid in the white man's tobacco field, I've beaten you at everything that you thought that you were superior at so you feel that to have all of the capability that I have, it would have to be my life's ambition to be white, can't you see, you brought me out of Africa, one of the strongest, most powerful, most intelligent people on the earth, and I can do anything that I want to do with God's help. Black people know who their enemy is. Slave masters didn't care that his slaves were sleeping on straw on the ground in cabins and huts. The only thing they had to wear was self-made shirts made from burlap croaker sacks. Pants and dresses were made from patches of anything they could find, never had anything new and never had anything to ever look forward to except hard work so that the whites could dress in the finest clothes and shoes, hats and saddles.

We all have seen depictions of the slave brief appearances in old South and western war movies. Understandably no black people produced movies that white studio and TV stations owners want to show. Black people want the nice cars and houses with money in the bank that you have, there is not one black person on earth that I ever heard of wanted to be white. The black people who use skin lightener are only doing that to get a good job in your companies and TV stations. It is one of the greatest insults in the world for a white person to not ask but suggest confidently that a black person wants to be white. There is nothing inferior about my skin color, it is perfect for me and where I came from. I remember reading Fredrick Douglas book in College, the life and times of (F.D), he said that on his first meeting with Abraham Lincoln, accompanied by Booker T. Washington when he was trying to convince Lincoln to let the black slaves fight for their freedom as the white Americans fought for their freedom in the American Revolution. Abe Lincoln looked Fredrick in the eye and told him that you and I are too far apart to ever come together or see eye to eye on anything, your features are far too different, suggesting that Fredrick was not human. Lincoln told him that he would be willing to support the venture of sending all Negroes back to Africa and finance a State in the country for that like Liberia, whose first name was Monrovia after President Monroe. Lincoln had absolutely no intention of ever freeing any slaves in any State until it was clear that if he didn't the Union would lose the war for certain, the Southern Confederates were kicking the Union in the back and in the front, on the left and on the right! The North was losing so badly that the Union soldiers and Generals were reluctant to go into battle. They couldn't win a single battle, and that's what it finally came down to when Pres. Lincoln realized that the only chance he had of turning the war around was to win one battle so that he could emancipate the slaves and send in the black troops after he heard about the successful battles being won by the 1st & 2nd South Carolina, all black volunteers under General Thomas Wentworth Higginson on November 3rd 1862, the St Mary' expedition. The Union Headquarters were located at Hilton Head South Carolina Commanded under General David Hunter. The runaway volunteer black union soldiers were successful before the 9th and 10th Calvary was ever formed in Boston Massachusetts Footnote "Firebrand- Liberty", Hilton head is where my ancestors came from, today the Graves Bridge crosses into Hilton Head Island. General Rufus Saxton of Beaufort South Carolina issues his "Emancipation Proclamation" in November 1862, but it was struck down by President Lincoln until he could get the credit for doing it himself after one of his Generals Ulysses S. Grant won a major battle. The slaves in South Carolina had been working in the fields by day and running away by night to the North. They brought information on the locations and camps, hide outs of the confederate soldiers, where their horses were kept, they cut them loose and ran them away while the soldiers slept since the first shot was fired on Fort Sumter. Every black man woman and child who was big enough became a Union spy. They set fires to Cotton gins, burned tobacco barns full of curing tobacco so that the slave owner wouldn't have money to escape after abandoning their property. The slaves went into the great mansions that they had worked for years to build and support and burned them down to the ground. Many slaves stayed on the property and farmed crops, and then bought the land. My family migrated.

CHAPTER FOUR

African American Adaptation In America

From Hilton Head to Georgetown to Britton's neck in Marion County. They worked and later moved to Rains and bought the farm.

My Dad lost his farm in the late fifties and we moved a few times until he got a job working on the railroad and Mom got a job in Marion at a clothing factory. We'll get back to the Civil War in later chapters but "Attention Reader" I 'm going to discuss everything so buckle up!

Footnote: Fire brand of liberty by—Stephen V. Ash

At mutual of Omaha where I worked for ten years I was the only black who made it successfully. The Division office manager often told me to talent scout another black to keep me company because none of his hiring of blacks panned out, none made it so I hired this little black guy three or four times because I enjoyed helping him and most of all, drinking with him when the office staff had banquets, Cookouts, picnics and parties. I engaged in conversations with the whites about everything freely and I really got to know most of them, they weren't used to dealing with a black man like me so I educated them fully, some men are Eagles and some are sparrows, I'm the Eagle at the top of the pack! No fear.

Going back to my teen years in high school at an all black school I got my education about white people in the tobacco field. The same people that I discussed in my previous book, Overcoming Obstacles in the South are the boys that I swam against and wrestled with in the field and always defeat, talked about sexual activity which was disgusting to me then and disgusting to me know, oral sex. I've always been proud of who I was and I realized that many black people preferred to be white than black and preferred to be light skinned than dark skinned. I'm sad to say that much of that hasn't changed but I'm certainly glad that it has evolved for the good in the thinking of most black people. Make no mistake there are a lot of Niggers around who want to be lighter or white. The light skinned kids were automatically treated better in school and other places as well. Those dark skinned people are the ones who do not know who they are, the ones that I call sparrows. I've been discriminated against by light skinned and dark skinned adults growing up, but worst by the darker skinned people in most cases. Before I began to interact with white boys in the tobacco fields I had never heard of or thought of such grossness as oral sex. Today most will curse you out if you say that you don't like it, well I've been married for forty years, tried it once when I was drunk and woke up and denied to myself that I never did that, no, I do not like or engage in oral sex! The white guy and I became reasonably close but never trusted him, that's the first thing that I was taught, never trust white people, they do not think of you as equal and they do not love you! I saw the white guy, and forgive me for using the white fraise but just keeping it real, that's the way that I refer to Caucasians under normal circumstances if they are around me are not. I do not hate any white people I've always found it too depressing to be angry and to be against anyone I chose to be for me and my efforts. The Atom bomb had to be dropped to keep America safe but I was not going admit that when I was conversing with the white guy that day in the restaurant. I saw him many years later after I left Mutual of Omaha companies; he too used to tell me, Ed I can take your wife from you since you don't believe in oral sex, I said if you can take my wife for that reason, then she doesn't belong to me anyway, and by the way she doesn't like it either. When I saw him years later he had been divorced three times and the woman who was living with him had just left him, I said hey boy, you boy, come here boy I guest your tongue must not be working!

In 1969 The Famous James Brown produced the record, I'm black and I'm proud and changed the world's thinking, black and white people woke up. That same year I took the hiatus from school and went to live in Baltimore for a year. The Navy recruiter told me to take some time and date some girls and when you're ready to go to England for the nuclear training come on back so I did. One night I went to a night club and many of the clubs were mixed and right out of the blue this white girl started to come on to me strongly and I accommodated her, something that I'd said that I would never do. I said I'm going to war in Vietnam and could possibly get killed so what the he--. I was twenty and she was nineteen years of age, good looking and was attending the University of Maryland. Well she spent the night, Friday, then Saturday because she wanted to go see the black movie "Halls of Anger" with me, trust me I didn't know, I thought everything was cool between blacks and whites in the North. We went downtown on the bus to Baltimore Street and when we got to the theater

45

there was a long line almost two blocks long. As I said she was a looker so the whites stared at me as we walked by going to the end of the line, but suddenly I walked by six or seven beautiful black girls, some caramel colored, some red bone, some dark and I must tell you when you find a really beautiful dark skinned woman, "God dog boy" she is out of sight!!! The young ladies stepped out of the line and surrounded us, "I know that a fine man like you are not out here with this white trash"! Everybody turned around and looked at us, mainly me, I told the white girl, let's go, I took her to the bus stop and I took off, never did get to see the movie. I saved some money in Baltimore and went back to Morris College, I could pay my bill then and the female President of the student body started talking about boycotting the dining hall, as much trouble as I had been having getting my meal tickets before I left school for Baltimore.

I have never tried to fit in with any group except at Church, I always looked and observed the Eagles in any gathering, my Grandfather told me where I was supposed to be and if my type wasn't there I was in the wrong place, many times son you must walk alone; When I was four I found out what my purpose in life was-which was placed in my heart by God in my mother's womb, we call it our dream, most times you have to see someone operating in the realm of your dream in order for you to discover it. When I graduated from Morris College in 1972 there were no business Degrees offered at the time. I worked in the school system for seven years and even though my parents were proud of me being the second in my family to graduate from College. A generation is forty years; it was expressed in our Bible when Moses led the slaves out of Egypt and they roamed for forty until that generation of slave mentality died. King David ruled for forty years as did Solomon forty years, a generation. An individual is always in the middle of their generation, those who are twenty years older and those who are twenty years younger are in your generation. My generation is the first from slavery who had the advantage of choice. If you didn't like the jobs available to you, you had the choice to change professions. The job in the school system was safe you could teach or be principal until retirement, the problem that I had was too many bosses and the salary was set, there was a cost of living and evaluation increase which was always minimal, I was always just getting by. If I needed a set of tires for my car I had to plan a month in advance and then I could only afford to buy two tires at once. There was always a line at the credit union or bank and all of us wound up at the grocery store the same time on Thursday or Friday when we got paid. We all bought gas at the same time. When I chose to go into the insurance business to work in the beginning for commission, you wouldn't believe how many people told me that I was a complete fool! You see, the first month that I graduated and got a job I went directly to the library and begun to educate myself in the business world and Metaphysics the study of all living things. When I was prepared I chose insurance because I found out that the whole world is financed by insurance, everything we buy and ever own has to be insured and the insurance companies houses the banks, which have to be insured. There are 2,500 insurance companies and none of them has ever gone broke. Another company will always bail or buy them out. I picked a company with presence and prestige that offered both Life and health insurance. A large company in the top five companies in the world Mutual and United of Omaha and they owned the wild Kingdom show (King). Presidents club was at the top with chairman's council for the big boys who had been in the business for several years. If you made presidents club for twenty years you were guaranteed to be a millionaire, I made presidents club for ten years consecutively, earning chairman's council two of those years. I utilized all of the sales training schools and got to meet some very impressive people. I never had to knock on any doors cold calling it was not my style to just show up at someone's door unannounced. We worked as the Doctors and Lawyers do by appointment only. Payday was on Tuesdays when there was no crowds at the banks and grocery stores. My unit manager told me that his previous job was manager of Kroger and the A&P stores and it was common practice nationwide for all prices on major sales products, meats can goods all of the popular basic products, eggs etc. He said that I had relaxed the tension in the office and everyone was happy that I was aboard, they were learning new things from me about black people. They thought that all black people were niggers and victims, always wanting a handout and someone two give them something. He said that on Wednesdays at or by twelve o'clock all of the prices were changed because black people all got paid on Thursdays and Fridays and they would pay a higher price Thursday, Friday, Saturday and Sunday. Black people were always broke on Mondays which allows the white people to pay a better price, he said just go into any grocery store on Monday or Tuesday, you will see two or three old white ladies, the Sothern white hunt deer and fish for most of their food, this guy was a true blue Yankee! I learned that the white man is always thinking about the black man and how to separate him from his money. Black people pay rent-late, light bill-late, phone bill and etc. late charges to make the whites richer without doing anything but waiting on the black people to pay the bills and late chargers, late; There's no reason to be angry at the white man he has been in charge from the beginning and he watches customs. I used to always wait until Mondays to buy suits and other clothes because there was no one in the store and all I had to do was ask for a deal every time I was truly impressed by some of the homes that I entered and one thousand acre ranches in Aiken sc. and other places Beautiful landscapes and just flowing with wealth. I learned something's but as soon as I left that property with a two or three thousand dollar check which ninety percent of it was mine as soon as I got to the office, no waiting, no taxes. I learned to realize that the house would never offer me comfort or pleasure and could never help me or make me happy in anyway, only your house can give you pleasure and no one loves your house but you! When I saw a multimillion dollar home I was not impressed, I always wanted a spacious, beautiful home for me and my family and I also wanted a second Sumer home near myrtle beach with a pool and a lake. I'm almost there at age 63 and a happy man. When the guys from the office and I went out for cocktails what always surprised me was that any of them were eager to buy for the whole party, something that I was not accustomed to I was genuinely impressed. Never have I experienced a brother offering to pay for my drink or my meal, except one, my brother Coby Deed. Ninety five percent of my clientele was white, Japanese or Chinese restaurant owners and other business owners. The first week in the business I realized that I was without any doubt going to flunk out the business dealing with black people, thirty percent of the population and twenty nine percent were broke. They told me to come back when I get paid or when I get my income tax check, guest what? what? They always hid in their own homes. Not home! I truly enjoyed the insurance business working two or three hours two or three days per week, it really gave me the opportunity to think, my favorite thing to do. Some years after I left the companies to start my own business I went to work for Xerox as a business consultant and training manager. I got fired after a couple of years though, I was in charge of making sure that there was a sales person at the best buys and office max stores for the copiers and printers. Boredom captured my mind as I was not really interested in working for anyone but myself at this stage (ON TTRACC INC.) and the rest is history in February 2013 I've made plans to build my beach home.

In the 60's 1965 the white farmers were enjoying the wealth from tobacco and cotton crops and cheap black labor, there were simply no other jobs other than farm work, the State Government was dead set on keeping the black people broke with their earnings from cropping tobacco to be spent in the local stores all over the South. No industry was allowed in South Carolina-car dealer ships etc. the only revenue they were interested in was tourism, no high paying jobs for blacks. Well the federal wage law was passed for five dollars per hour. The white farmers were outraged they weren't about to pay black boys and girls forty dollars per day to work in their tobacco and cotton. The farmers had relative's downtown owning department stores; the wealth was always in a cycle, farmer pay black laborers six dollars per day and they went downtown on Fridays and spent all of it, got broke and went back into the fields on Monday morning come rain or shine. The farmers rebelled by purchasing expensive farm equipment, tobacco and cotton harvesters for three and four hundred "thousand" dollars each. They had not thought about the monthly payments for the machinery was going to be mailed out of State which were huge. It gave the blacks the opportunity to get jobs in local factories and also move out of State for better jobs. There was no money being generated downtown in any of the stores so they went under. The farmers went broke because they borrowed money on the land that had been in their families for two and three hundred years. I saw them on ETV often saying that they were going to have to seek employment at the McDonalds and Burger Kings because none in the white families had ever considered sending their children to Colleges they had farms to past down and inherit. There was a Hardees, two McDonalds in Marion in the 1980's a Kentucky fried chicken and a Maryland fried chicken- population 45,000 and 95% black. Today there is one KFC in Mullins eight miles east of Marion, no Hardees and no Maryland chicken and one of the McDonalds has closed. All of the black people who were young enough to leave have left the building. Marion has the highest Unemployment rate in the State, it was 24% at one time and now it is an embarrassment to the public so it is not announced on the news anymore.

When Obama won the election in November 2012, today is the twenty seventh of November and they just finally accounted for the last two hundred and forty votes and looking for someone to fire. The election was held on November 6th.

Victimized And Big Payback

On a slave plantation the stories told to me were "horrific", the slaves were made to work from can to can't- meaning they worked from first daylight as soon as they could see until the day was so dark until you couldn't see anything. When the quitting time was sounded all slaves went into their cabins, the men carried in the chopped wood for the women to cook super after a long days work on a wood burning stove. The children gathered water from the stream or well for cooking and bathing, the mass' a has already had his meal prepared by his house niggers, he's had his juleps and other cocktails and cigars by five o'clock in the evening. The slave driver has retired to his evening of pleasure with one of the hands young daughters for the night. Now that all power and supervision has abated and gone, the slaves are free to return to being proud to be black, whereas all during the daylight hours when the slaves are out and about in the fields and barns, no slave wants to be black, it is taboo to be black and a slave because there is no place for a black person to hide and they are considered to be inhuman, with no feelings of sadness, loneliness or pride in America. The slave master uses a didactic approach to the methodology of victimizing his slaves, he takes the young boys ages twelve through twenty and directs them to work details alongside men who are forty five and over. This is a certain imbalance in working ability both in strength and endurance. The slave master shows up periodically to brag and motivate the younger group while he curse and expresses derogatory criticisms of the older men whom he has worked almost to death the exact same way years earlier. He then takes the light skinned boys whom he and his slave driver has sired and reproduced, pulled them to the side and give them a fried chicken leg each while giving the young black boys chicken necks or backs and giving the old men one piece of fat back and corn bread. The light skinned boys are constantly treated as if they are almost white and the dark skinned slaves are treated as if they are less than the light skinned slaves, pitting the one against the other is the mentality carried over through slavery and after the slavery. After I drew upon this analogy I understood where the white guy was coming from when he suggested boldly and assuredly that he knew that I wanted to be white even after I was leading thirty white business men in sales production and everything else in our office. My Uncle told me that the slave owner would allow his young sons to have a male slave their same age to play and practice on. After they compete in wrestling and foot racing and such and the slave believes that this white boy is his good friend, the owner would tell his sons to go down to the slave boy's mama's cabin, tell the black woman's husband to go outside and wait until he practices having sex with the black slave's wife and the black boy's Mama's.

Pay back comes in many different forms over time when the slave owner doesn't realize how he has hurt the boy and his Dad. The slaves past the word around as to what has transpired and indicate to all that the same thing will happen to them one day, the pay back process begins. The white slave master has an assistant, one who use to be a great worker but now he is old, depending on how large the plantation is there will be two assistants one young and old. The assistant slave is a great actor, a superb step and fetch it! When planting time comes next spring the fix is on, when the fields are prepared for planting and the rows are bedded, the fertilizer is only put down at the ends of the rows about twenty feet into the row, the fertilizer is not placed on top of the bed of the row where the seeds go, the fertilizer is put down in the middle where man and the mule walks, only grass will grow-not the seeds. When the seeds come up and the grass outgrow the plants the white master order the plowing to begin. The slaves during the plowing have been trained by the black slave driver who consequently remembers that Massa has sold off two or three of his wives after abusing them sexually. Sold off several of his children both on this plantation and on other plantations that Massa has hired him out to breed with another slave owner's female slaves for money, just like a Bore hog is hired out to breed and grow a crop of hogs for the other man. The cotton, tobacco, corn wheat and every crop is stunted and useless for market. The slaves cut openings in fences so that the slave owner's cattle and hogs can constantly get out and go on another plantation owner's farm causing damages that the Massa will have to pay out of pocket. The slaves are eating very good without Massa knowing a thing. The next year Massa has to borrow more and more money from the banks until he is almost bankrupt, the slaves start to run to the east and to the west where ever the Union soldiers are located. Run before Massa realizes that he has to sell off some slaves to get out of debt. All slaves knew this process, as long as Massa treated the slaves moderately well. Outside of the cabin the slave wanted to be white or any other color that was not black because of the horrific treatment but as soon as the slave got out of the sight of the slave master, "shoot" the heck with being white, no one is greater than the black man when he is free, in his own cabin! The slave owner knew nothing about what went on in the middle of his fields, only what he could see on the ends of the rows. Rows were very long to maximize the land's production. There were concoctions that the slave could mix up to make the mules, hogs and cows sick from weeds moss and grasses from the woods, just mix it up in the feed at night! The cooks inside the house used crushed glass ground up and put in Massa's food which would slowly kill him. They knew how to mix poisons from herbs and mushrooms which would be undetected by local Doctors who were summoned to come out. The slaves knew many ways to pay you back if you did them wrong, and it was very easy for them to pretend that they loved you Massa, we sick Massa? The slave owner never knew what was on the slave's mind but the slave always knew exactly what the Master was thinking. When they ran to the Union soldiers camp they told where everything was, what time Massa went to bed and what time he awakened each day. They told them where the Gold coins and money, rifles and all other weaponry was kept. How much tobacco and cotton was stored before taking it to market, and when it was supposed to be transported and go back to the plantation before daylight, go to bed and work in the fields the next day until the Union soldiers were prepared to raid. I understood early in life that whites thought that all blacks wanted to be white, however after the schools were integrated and the whites saw that the things that their parents told them about blacks were not true, in the 1980's he still thinks that I wanted to be white, I was totally blown away and still am.

CHAPTER FIVE

The Word Nigger vs. Cracker

In 1979, the year that I went to work for the Mutual of Omaha Companies I expressed to the all-white staff and sales force openly that I was prepared and welcomed any conversation to discuss everything that anyone wanted to talk about. I'm impervious to the word Nigger, it does not affect me negatively, I know who I am and proud to be so. In eighty percent of black and white homes in America the word Nigger is used freely by both races. Black people use the word in fun and jesting while white people use the word as a weapon against blacks. The word Cracker is used in eighty percent of black households as a means of distrust. "Cracker" is the word blacks use to combat the word Nigger but the two words do not carry the same "power", when a white person is called cracker it has absolutely no effect because he or she believes that black people will always be inferior! I'm six feet tall weighing three hundred solid pounds, no fat stomach, I'm a trained boxer and if a five foot two man called me a chump, it would have relatively no effect at all. It is time that we as black people redefine the word Nigger and embrace it, it is never going to go away and I welcome that as fact.

NIGGER: A nigger is a person or people who have been enslaved, victimized, belittled and in spite of all nefarious (crooked) treatment still perseveres and rises to the top in a land that was not there's.

(B) The nigger loves, believes in and trust his God above all "OBAMA". During the raids of the 1st and 2nd South Carolina black runaway slaves, the white officers sent written reports to President Lincoln stating that the black soldiers were easier to train and caught on more quickly than the white soldier because of their natural inherent rhythm. When the black soldiers herd the rhythm of the sound of officers counting one, two, three, four with sounds of footsteps in unison it was relative to the sound of the drum in Africa. Some white officers discriminated against the black soldiers at first, sighting that the nigger was listless, no good for battle and would throw down their weapons at the first sign of battle but General Higginson was vigilant and replaced the white officers with black sergeants. Once the black officers took command it was all she wrote, the two black regiments went into battle at the ST. Mary's raid on the Islands of Amelia, St. Helena and wiped out the Confederate soldiers, a great defeat and successful attack in the South Carolina. General Thomas W. Higginson realized in that battle which he saw with his own eyes the fearlessness of the black runaway slaves. Let me hip you right here, right now, no matter how badly you treat black people, after they realized that God had given them their first chance to set their wives and children free forever, death is much better than living on their hands and knees as a slave. The slaves saw what their grandparents and Great grandparents had prayed for, sweated and sometimes worked themselves to death for and they jumped and danced they shouted for joy as never before and the white officers could not understand it. After long drills work details and practice, they drilled some more and after the drills were done they celebrated religiously celebrated some more until bedtime. But before sunrise they were up and ready to go into battle again. It was a great payback for all of the bad treatment that they endured for hundreds of years. The black slaves were a tribal people and hand to hand combat was second nature to them, the white slave traders did not know who it was that they were stealing and capturing to belittle brain wash and reduce a powerful people such as they to become permanent servants. No one was willing to fight for their freedom as the slave himself. The Southern confederates, even the poor whites who never owned a single slave, wanted to be white and rich in America. Rich, famous and then comes the need for power. Did the slaves want to be white when they stepped outside their cabins, "yes", and so did the poor whites and all of the other immigrants who came to America and are still coming. White Americans are the most powerful people on the Earth, America is the most powerful Country in the Universe and everyone wants that power, it is the way of the world since the beginning of time. But make no mistake, African Americans want the good life that the wealth and power brings but they want those things in black hands. There are no pictures of a white Jesus hanging in the homes of Ninety percent of the black people in America today, the bottom has come to the top, bottom rail has evolved.

Every country in the universe has patterned itself after "Rome", the names of cities-every city in America has a Greenville, a Marion county and the like, that is the way that it was in Rome two thousand years ago. Rome had all of the modern essentials that we enjoy all over the world today, the postal system, the welfare system-running water, inside bathrooms etc. Rome conquered northern Africa and built the modern city of Timgad with running water and inside toilets two thousand years ago.

They had a citizenship process that existed where after you served twenty five years in the military you received your citizenship card written in stone. Paved streets and all, the black Africans voluntarily submitted to the Roman authorities and joined the military and became Roman citizens in their own country of North Africa, now what the Romans got out of the deal was a powerful fighting force of African soldiers, that's why Rome had such a strong military force for four hundred years. No one seems to have any idea why Rome fell, well why didn't you ask me? They killed God's son, Jesus Christ by Pontius Eurileius Pilate.

The Roman soldiers developed a secret society of Christians, after they spied on Jesus ministry for three and a quarter years and saw with their own eyes the miracles that he performed they decided that he had a power that truly did not come from earth but above; The night they went to arrest Jesus in the garden, footnote: St. John the 18th chapter and the fifth verse, Jesus asked "whom do you seek, who are you looking for, when the Roman soldiers answered and said "Jesus of Nazareth, when he said, "I am he" all of the soldiers fell backwards to the ground and stayed as dead men until all twelve of Jesus disciples escaped. They saw Jesus feed the five thousand and when the Roman centurion came to Jesus and asked him to just say the word that his servant would be healed and he knew that it would be so, many were convinced became Christians and worshiped in secrecy until the Government of Rome came tumbling down! Historically African warriors are supreme since the earth began however we have been in trouble with God many times and consequently enslaved many times. The trouble is that after hundreds of years past and no one remembers the days when the black Africans were a great and powerful people, go pick them up put them in bondage and never know when God is coming to set his people free. Ceaser Augustus built the city of Timgad in North Africa.

Many times over the years I saw the movie starring Rock Hudson and John Wayne at the ending of the Civil War where Rock Hudson was abandoning his plantation to escape the wrath of the Union soldiers and also have to live in a country of the New America where the black slaves were as free as he was. Every time that I see the red confederate flag, I laugh because to me it represents the ass kicking the runaway slaves put on the bearers of that flag. Yes, it was the black runaway slaves who won the Civil War. The slaves in Charleston and Beaufort knew every inch of the territory of each plantation and island in the lower State. When the slaves heard through the grape vine that the Union soldiers were coming to South Carolina they started planning and stealing axes, hatches and any other thing that they could find to fight with. They dug canals and trenches in the woods and covered them up with branches and pine straw to hide both themselves and the Union soldiers when the fighting started. The cooks and maids in the big houses listened closely at everything that was said around dinner tables and at the big plantation parties that were held with invited guest from all over the South and the North. Valuable information that would aid the Union soldiers when the time came. It was a time of great excitement in the fields when no whites were around. In the cabins at night the plans to run were made as soon as they saw the first blue uniforms. Everyone on plantations began to lay the step and fetch it acts on thick. Everyone except one or two slaves on a plantation would play act as dumb as a box of broken hammers all of the time anyway.

The dumber you acted the less tough chores you were asked to do. Anyway that you could get out of doing the torturous back breaking work on the farm that's just what you did, who cares how often you are degraded if it got you out of the free labor. The slave owner ate steak, pork chops fried chicken and the only chicken parts he wanted were the white meat, breast and wings e gave the short thighs and backs to the cooks and maids. The slaves ate fat back, neck bones hog head and feet. They had to make their own soap from the fat from the hog. Black people today or much more Prone and likely to develop high blood and diabetes than whites. Many black men are still afraid to go to white Doctors because of the terrible treatment and experimentation they performed on blacks in the past. Being used as guinea pigs is practiced in rural areas today. There are rules that were past down from generation to generation as to how to stay alive and stay healthy, many ways to slow a mule down and keeping him from over working you when a knew young energetic mule is brought to the farm. The slave master always put an older male to work-breaking in the new mule. First the old guy would introduce himself as master of the mule and if the mule did not obey there would be consequences such as taking the bit and file it into Sharpe points in the middle and on both ends which causes pain to the mule in the mouth when he is turned to the left or right. The plow lines would be criss crossed under the throat and wrapped around the plow handles tightly so that there would be no slackness.

When I was around ten or eleven I was conducting on the work station that we called drag driver, the croppers in the tobacco field would place the leaves into the drag which was made of two flat two by four boards used as rudders to slide on the ground and there were coverings on the sides made from burlap croaker sack bags. When we finished one field in the morning my friend and I got to ride to the next field which was six miles away on dirt roads. Well it just so happened that I was given the smaller stubborn ugly mule. Everyone else went on ahead of us and went to lunch because it was that time and anyone who has had dealings with a mule knows that a mule is not dumb as he may look, they will not work past the noon hour without their noonday feeding. We climbed up on our mules with the intention of transporting them to the next field and then feed them. Ridge climbed up first and then I hopped up on my mule. This crazy mule started to buck gently at first to throw me off balance and at the same time he was bouncing me backwards towards the hips end parts and when he had me squarely on his hips he bucked furiously and powerfully throwing me way up in the air and I landed flat on my back knocking every ounce of air out of my lungs. I was squirming on the ground trying to catch my breath for what seemed like an eternity groaning and when I caught a glimpse of the mule he was just turned around looking at me as if to say you should have known better! Ridge was scared and didn't know what to do so he just bends over looking at me with freight. Ooowe, when I was able to catch my breath I was a very happy camper, I thought that I had broken my back. I was very angry at that stupid mule for trying to hurt a kid like me for only ridding him. I locked my heels in behind his front shoulders and let him have it on both sides with the plow lines. Ridge had a bigger and faster mule so he told me to hit him between the ears Arvanie and boy was that effective. This little slow mule stretched out beneath me as I had never felt any mule or horse ever do before, he passed my friend and kept getting it until we arrived at the other farm, he ran so fast until all I heard was four rapid foot clod ding on the road as the wind past my ears loudly. It was exciting! Many things have brought both happiness and sadness over my life time. Ps. The Mule and the donkey are the only two animals that are able to see "all four feet at the same time" making them the sure footed creations.

Happiness VS Sadness

Over the years I have observed and read the life stories of rich and famous people describe their life experiences as being a "great ride", Life has been very rewarding and they wouldn't change a thing if they had the chance. I'm 63 years old and I've made many changes and adjustments in my life and if I could there are a lot of changes that I would make if I could. Frankie Beverly the rhythm and blues singer recorded a hit record titled "Joy and pain," and I'm in total agreement with the way that the Universe is. I was very saddened when I decided to leave Mutual of Omaha and start my own Insurance Agency in 1988 and found my Division Office Manager had taken almost all of my deferred compensation money just to keep me in his employ. First he froze it and then he took it, while he was already a very rich man, it all evolves back to the thinking of the whites having this idea that all African Americans are inferior, that we need and love for them to take care of us and our money throughout life. Sadness is when our children are the first generation who are experiencing life to be less rewarding as their parents because of recessions and depressions. Sadness is having to realize that our daughters will not enjoy the happy companionship of marriage because too many of our young black men are dying or in prison and youngest black men have too many children by the time they reach the age of twenty. When I was a young man-all of the brothers told us to get all of the women that you can while you can, even black Dads said that same foolish thing. Sadness is when you witness your friends die young or more importantly parent having to bury their own children. Sadness is working all of your life only to watch your savings dwindle because of escalating gas prices anytime oil companies decide to give themselves a raise and the cost of living expenses in general. Sadness is when you cut your grass on Friday and it rains on Saturday, Sunday, Monday through Thursday and have to cut again on Friday ha ha.

Happiness: there was a time when I was doing research on the differences in the purposes of individuals lives and chosen professions. I ask myself what is the purpose of a comedian? Telling jokes just to make others laugh and make a very good living doing it. Well I got a huge slap in the face when I discovered that the doctors who study and operate on the brain have determined that when an individual laughs their brain releases serotonin all throughout the body and causes a healing and coating effect for the organs and prevent cancer! It is a known fact that one can heal themselves by surrounding themselves with friends who can make them laugh daily. It is one of the reasons I believe so heavily in class and family reunions, everyone knows that as soon as you see each other the first thing that happens before the hugs is great laughter. When you are constantly angry at someone or something it depresses you a lot more than you realize and it causes the opposite effect, stress causes your body organs to weaken and deteriorate, Serotonin heals and protects the body from other diseases as well. One day I asked the question? What about being hen pecked, how difficult is that to avoid? An older gentleman spoke right up before someone said something stupid, he said there is absolutely nothing wrong with being henpecked if you are being henpecked by the right hen.

Happiness is when you realize that at the moment of conception four to five million sperm cells are released by the male into the womb of the woman and God selects only one and give it the power to swim faster and accurately to connect with the egg, causes fertilization and birth. Millions died so that we could live and come into the world, so we were all winners the moment we were born. We have been given the power to overcome obstacles beyond measure; it's just a matter of searching until you find the right solution. I make it a priority to forgive and never hold on to anger it simply takes too much of your energy to force yourself to stay angry with someone. Anger and hate will destroy you from within, when I feel overwhelmed with stress or anger I go to the nearest lake or beach, water has a calming effect, it is why Jesus did seventy five percent of his teachings either on or near water. Water helps you to channel and capture good positive thoughts.

The parades in Marion and Mullins brought me much happiness during the fall of the year each time I returned to my hometown. Bands blasting with drums and horns, dancing in the street, the world seems to belong to the young at heart but decisions have to be made with care. Just like a problem or obstacle will expand when you think about it negatively, it will expand the same way for good if you think about it positively. King Solomon said that money answered (changes) all things no matter what you are doing or thinking about doing when money or the prospect of wealth shows up in your life, immediately you begin to feel better and happier. Serotonin kicks in and sprinkles all over your body inside and there is a healing effect which causes growth in the right direction.

In 1701 during the industrial revolution Antoine M. "Cadillac" founded the city of Detroit in the State of Michigan, he opened a fur trading business and his descendants developed the name into an automobile giant, Nephews William Durant founded General motors and William Murphy backed the young Henry Ford a mechanic for General motors' along with Louis Chevrolet. Those people chose new and innovative ideas and just look where it has taken them at this juncture. Most black people that I know aren't associates or relatives of anyone who has the financial standing to step in and fund a viable idea or project yet but it is coming. More and more young black multi-millionaires are crossing that threshold every year, God is finding strange ways to get wealth into the hands of the children of former slaves and there's nothing that anyone can do about it. It is time now' just hold on to your dreams and it will show up in the form of wealthy ideas. Antoine De-Lamothe Cadillac (footnote) World book encyclopedia); From France, gave himself the name along with some royalty status, he faked it until he made it. There are young Hip hop artist whom I'm proud to say are owning their own record labels and creating their own drinks and clothing lines, perfumes etc. Belief in yourself will get you a lot further in life than just getting a job that you don't like and because it pays well you remain on that job unhappy for thirty or forty years and die too soon because of stress! Wealthy hip hop artists are funding the businesses of associates because they have it, my generation do not.

More and more legislators are showing up with black skin, in Mississippi the most prejudice State in the United States of America has evolved into a State which has more black public officials than any other State, wake up "it's time now". No prices are going to come down for the good stuff, only the stuff that never sells anyway, what do you think that merchants and clothing stores do with the stuff that doesn't sell during the year? At the beginning of the New Year they have a blow-out sale and get all of your income tax money- oh yeah all businesses know how to attract black folks money when it shows up, they are waiting to have a sale, some of that money should be saved to start your own business next year you are never going to get enough clothes. And why do you think that there are so many used car dealers showing up with shinny cars during tax time. Every holiday there is a gas price hike, I said that's it I'll travel after the holiday. Every day I watch "Cops "it is the live show where you can turn to and see black people every day. In 1641 the police force was formed for free black people and they wonder why white people surveyed and interviewed always say they trust the police whereas black people distrust and run from the police when they see them coming. It is the policy of every State to get the fingerprints of every black person living in that State and the next thing is to place a felony arrest on each one to stop the "voting privileges" and the opportunity to get a decent job. The craziest thing that catches me off guard every time is when the police "white police" with all of the equipment around their waist can run faster and always catch the black person running and catch um'. The police take the liberty of parking a brand spanking new Escalade directly in the middle of the poorest black neighborhood and leave the keys within, make loud noises to draw attention to and get the attention of the black people who have absolutely nothing and use a bait car to arrest and place felonies on the record of young black people, as soon as the police catch them jumping out and running they ask? Why did you run? the police represent nothing but sadness to black people, they are taking them out of their homes away from their love ones, lock them up with a bail that they can't pay, a felony on their record which prevents them from getting gainful employment from rich white people and they ask? Why did you run?

The police use a female officer, dressed up in short shorts and go into the black neighborhood to in trap poor silly black people to get their hard earned money, place them in jail to pay court cost and bail. It is time now to wake up!

It has often brought me sadness when I ventured to think about others who have achieved under dire circumstances and terrible obstacles and accomplish great and meaningful things in their lives. Fredrick Douglas was born a slave yet he broke free under his own power and started his own Newspaper, wrote books and advised US. Presidents, became a US. Marshall and after all of that he built and owned a twenty room house in Washington DC.

I was born a free man, owned cars early in life obtained a college Education and I still struggled seemingly as much as he did to get where I wanted to be. It is my intention though to finish with my life of this world happy and when I step over into the invisible world of spirit and go to the welcoming banquet with my thoughts intact and be certain that I have used every idea possible, and used every phase of my physical strength to do and to help everyone that I can to do more as well. When I think about the very successful people who die young surprisingly it doesn't sadden me because I accept the fact that they have successfully completed their life's work. Michael Jackson, Elvis Pressley, Tupac and Sam Cooke etc. However King David was blessed to have it both ways, God Said that he was a man after his own heart. Through meditation and fervent prayer I have come to realize that it is not how holy we try to live, it is how much we can "learn to love God". The Bible says that the greatest thing that we can do is to love God with all of our hearts, all of our minds, all of our strength and all of our soul. The only way that we can love God under these specifications is to ask God to take control of our minds, our hearts, our soul and all of our strength and teach us to love him at that level. When David was a young boy growing up tending sheep all alone, the youngest of eight brothers, he had no friends in the wilderness all day everyday which gave him the opportunity to develop a wonderful relationship with nature and God. When God told David that he was going to deliver the giant who stood nine feet nine inches tall Goliath into his hands he also told him that Goliath had four brothers, a total of five so that's the reason why David picked up the five smooth stones at the brook. Goliath was the oldest of the brothers but not the largest! A giant has to be over eight feet tall; one was a little over thirteen feet tall. Samson was to my estimation six foot three or six foot four inches tall a normal man.

(Health) has always been very important to me and about twenty years ago a classmate of mine developed Colon Cancer; He had the operation and chemotherapy and all went well, today he is fine, he strongly suggested that I have a colon-ostraphy done because he had never had any adverse health issues, his weight was slender so I decided since it was free and I found out that it was a major cause of stomach cancer and it was listed under an exceptional death prevention rate simply by being informed. I was given a solution called Magnesium citrate, in a clear bottle, cost a dollar in the dollar store in raspberry and lemon flavor also. It was a solution that I had been introduced to by my sister in law about ten years earlier and I liked the results and relief that it gave me in exactly two hours after having two or more glasses of water over the two hour period and I didn't need to use it but two or three times per year. I was forty one years old when I took the colon ostraphy and to my surprise the Dr. found two pea size polyps on my colon (large intestine) and he relieved me of it with a laser. Now, several people in my immediate family have died of stomach and colon cancer, that was scary; The Dr. told me to keep my colon clean by using the same solution because the magnesium citrate was harmless, it's designed to work naturally with your body, shoot I like the bathroom anyway I have a small library in my bathroom, sometimes I have to be chased out for reading so long. We learned in high school that it takes only two hours to digest food after you have had your meal, consequently if your body acts properly which mine does not, after two hours you could get rid of the body waste right away but normally the food stays in your body all day and sometimes longer continuously cooking at 98.6% drying further. As soon as I realize that I have eaten two or three meals in one day and haven't visited the bathroom, gulp, gulp, gulp a half bottle of the solution and I feel just great.

CHAPTER SIX

Transition

Archeologist and historians both ancient and present continue to insist that they are seriously trying to discover who the people were five thousand years ago who were the builders of the great pyramids in Egypt. I've discussed earlier that the very name Egypt is taken from the Hebrew word in our Bible "Mizraim" which means Egypt, the second son of black Ham son of Noah. Whenever the evidence leads to the inhabitants being or having pure black skin, Historians say "there must be some mistake "no Niggers could have done this! However in "Machu Picchu" there is no question these were the Inca- Indians and at Stone Hedge, Europeans. Of course it doesn't even bother me anymore I'm writing the true history of Africans and African Americans all over the world and they are easy to find. After being slaves in Egypt we were enslaved again in Babylon and in 1526 the first known records exist for our slavery in America except this time God said that" it was time" and we have evolved into the White house, to the highest power in this land.

2012 the new millennium has exhibited a redistribution of wealth, terrible monetary losses through ponse-schemes, real estate schemes, gas price schemes, Bank bail outs after the great swindle. What has to happen now are black Business ownership and land purchases. Grocery stores are funded primarily by black people, we own almost no gas stations we own real estate offices, Ins. offices some clothing stores, Lourie's Men store on main street where I used to love to shop formally owned by Frank Lurie(white owned) has been replaced by India Indians. There is one magnificent black owned men clothing store behind Columbia Mall that I've shopped for over twenty years now, Fashions (2). Way to go Fashions! Life is exciting now when you know what to expect, tremendous breakthroughs are forth coming. The world no longer exists with just the white majority owning everything. Pick up your dreams it is time now. Business loans are still hard to get, car loans, they all exist because in 1945 when the black US. Soldiers came home from war and started buying homes in white neighbor hoods under the new GI Bill, white governing powers started the credit beacon scores for black people! So we have a police force started in Charleston South Carolina in 1641 for free black people and the credit scores started in 1946-47 for black people, unlocking secret obstacles in the South! If you are living from paycheck to paycheck quite obviously you are going to wind up paying expensive late fees for many things, late rent payments or house payments, late car and insurance payments etc. I remember when I was just starting out with a new bride and car payments I had a mobile home payment, I was getting paid bi-weekly, bought TV and phone. I knew that I was over my head with bills but I felt as though the world was my playground and I was going to learn how to play in it. I and my family wasn't going to suffer, Jesus said that his yoke was easy. When I cashed my paycheck my wife and I went directly to the grocery store immediately after I filled my cutlass up with gas. I knew that I had to think of everything in terms of bi-weekly which meant that I was only going to pay my bills in terms of urgency. When the bill collectors started calling I was not going to hide out in my own home so I answered each caller once and when they called back I just picked up the phone and laid it down on top of the TV to make sure that they understood that I was not going to give anyone's voice and audience after the first call when I instructed them when I would pay, next payday, I wasn't going to give anyone all of my money and live completely broke until my next payday. An individual feels completely useless when they are totally broke. I'm never going to be hungry more than a couple of hours and I'm never going to be completely broke, if I'm not fasting I will not go hungry. As I get older I don't eat very much because I certainly don't like exercise anymore. I take one twenty five mg. blood pressure pill and I have a black female Dr. whom I like and trust, I'm not Diabetic but all of my siblings are, I have sinus and seasonal allergies and I walk between four and six days per week with a thirty minute exercise routine at home, I don't like crowded exercise gyms I like walking in my own neighborhood. I have paid some high interest in the past but at the time I had to have what I wanted and I dealt with the consequences. I know that a prudent person shouldn't spend money on things that they can't afford but the way that I approached spending was what I learned from the insurance business, if I didn't have the money I could get on my phone and make some business calls and within two or three hours I made the money. During the seventies, eighties and nineties jobs were plentiful until the new millennium (2000) kicked in and the economic transition began, Companies closed or moved the jobs overseas for cheaper labor. During any transition stage there will be suffering for some people if adjustments aren't made in your thinking, the young men and women cannot find gainful employment sufficient for supporting an apartment or home purchase, therefore our grown children are staying at home with parents much longer these days.

In my early forties I realized that people don't just die from old age it is because we don't take care of our body organs inside. My Dr. recommended that I take a pre-diabetic course at one of our local Hospitals because Diabetes was very prevalent in my family history and the wealth of information was life saving. First of all I found out that one twelve once soda has ten teaspoonful of pure sugar, I was advised to stay away from all of the white foods, white flour, white rice, all white breads, all pasta and I found out that white milk is transmitting diabetes from the cow to humans, I quit all of the above except white rice which I've backed away from-some! I quit smoking at age thirty two and gained eighty pounds within six months. I could determine from riding down the street in my car if I was getting close to a KFC. Churches, Bo jangles or pop eyes chicken store. I was relatively young though, I had the energy to lose the weight within another six months. When I turned age forty five I quit drinking alcohol and guest what? Yeah ED we know, I gained one hundred pounds within six months and I've been struggling with the weight every since, I lose some and go right back and find it! I'll never quit though it's just a matter of me making up my mind to stick with my own program. You have to do something, anything for three to five days per week to make yourself tired enough to get your heart rate up for just a few moments. Be careful about putting anything in your body that it doesn't need, I once spoke with an old man who told me that if he knew that he was going to live as long as he did he would have taken much better care of his body, great advice for all of us. Too many strong medicines passing through your kidneys will obviously result in you developing kidney problems in your later years, if your body doesn't need it stop taking it, try the honey and lemon tea, a blessed food. All of these things have to do with unlocking secret obstacles. My Dr. (A. Stewt.) is great so many people love her until she hardly has time for a lunch break so guest what? I'm a great cook so periodically I grill ribs and chicken, cook seasoned rice and veggies for her, that gives me a no waiting deal on my check-ups. We are living longer because we are eating better and seeing our Dr., we are educating ourselves on our life styles and exercise, we are becoming aware of the fact that black people and other minorities are transitioning into a new way of life. The actor John Wayne died with around twenty five pounds of waste in his colon as did Elvis Pressley. It takes fourteen hours to digest an eight ounce steak, something that I love (rib eyes) and sirloin.

After I completed my studies at Morris College I was happy to be doing the things that mattered to me the most, I had read all of the books available on African and African American history in America. I wanted to know how long it would take the greatest minds and most powerful people on Earth to regain their status with God's help, the exact same thing that I wanted to know as a child. During the African slave trade enslaved Africans were transported and sold in North Africa, the Middle East, Persia, India, the Indian Ocean lands and in Europe, Russia, England Dutch and Portugal. The African has made everyone rich except himself all wealth in America has its roots in slavery. Footnote: Book titled, In Motion, African Migration Experience; The founders of America only took three hundred years to move from horse and mule drawn wagons in the early fifteen hundreds through the eighteen hundreds with slaves, if they did not treat us right what makes you think that the whites would ever teach us anything about building our own businesses and relying on our own schools. American Express, AT&T, Verizon, Xerox and all of the large giant companies, their founders have children, nieces, nephews and friends that they wish to give their top CEO' and COO's, Presidents VP'S and board Chairman's jobs to and I don't blame them it is the same thing that I want for my own family, your job title and position can change over a cocktail, or on the golf course any day. It is not just happen-stance that the gas prices keep rising and falling, companies closings and moving, the actuaries and planners have already made decisions about our futures fifty and one hundred years from now. Our children are the first generation since slavery who can expect to earn a lesser productive lifestyle than their parents. We do not know any friend or family member who can give us a business startup loan or job that will pay our children six figure salaries at any time in the future. There is a very simply reason why the economy failed and the housing crises puts minorities further back into the ghettos than they were before they purchased the underwater houses, some middle class whites got caught in the net but it was a planned result. The rich are able to come along and buy property cheap anytime there is a downturn in the economy. Any time you are working on someone else's job for a set salary trading your time and efforts for dollars punching a clock, trust me you're never going to make enough money. (Late payments) make other people rich without doing a thing. In 2008 we all saw President Obama print money and bail out the richest corporations on earth, no white President would have ever done that, Romney would have let them all go under and today we would have been experiencing Romney Motors instead of General Motors as it should be. The largest insurance company in the world would be-Romney INS. CO. of the world. Black people were not supposed to witness such a mighty and powerful act as that. Only God can do miracles such as we've seen. We saw centuries of a people come up from slavery, create their own language in a foreign land, from working days from can see until can't see. Raggedy clothes to suit walking up the steps of the white house to rule the greatest and most powerful country in the world. There are whites in South Carolina today who gave up their belief in God because they believed that the just God created black people for the supreme purpose of working and serving white people (justly) for all eternity. I've paid some high interest rates in my salaried years and couldn't do anything about it. On November 3, 1862 black runaway slaves in Charleston and Beaufort South Carolina worked in fields all day while they could see and ran at night when they couldn't see other than by moonlight. They completely took themselves from their white slave masters by unsuspecting means and left them wondering how and why would their darkies pick up and leave them when the slaves were supposed to love their masters so much. They left so smooth until the female Republican candidate is still fooled after having stories told to her by her ancestors that their slaves were fed fat back meat and given croaker sack shirts, pants and dresses to wear until they fell off of their bodies. Fed grits three times per day with just the fat back grease over the grits, Michelle Bachman is still angry that she don't have her slaves to look at waving at her everyday as she leaves for work in her Mercedes. I'm sure that it is downright painful for a lot of whites who had their slave property taken from them in the Civil War, they are still waiting for the South to rise again! Michelle Bachman- said black people were better off during slavery. That's like saying that America was better off with mules and wagons without cars and computers, some would give it all up if they could just have their slaves back.

Abraham Lincoln was forced into greatness and he admitted it himself when he was on the battle field at Antietam and Gettysburg, he saw twenty five thousand Union soldiers die While thirty two thousand Confederate soldiers die as well. He also told Fredrick Douglas to his face while looking directly into his eyes, he said that Fred you and I are too far apart to ever see eye to eye, referencing his broad nose and dark skin. The 1st and 2nd South Carolina went through their basic training with un-believable speed and accuracy, the supply commissary attendant sent them bright red pants so that they could be seen from miles away. They were subjected to inhumane degradation and constant cursing and Nigger this and Nigger that but still prevailed. After they successfully defeated the Rebel soldiers on the St. Mary's raid they went back to their former plantations where they had been slaves and freed the slave families they had left behind. They were quoted as saying" we are the ones who are freeing yawl," it is my hands set tin you free"! Afterwards they went back to Beaufort and had an Emancipation ceremony along with a parade down the streets of the town in Beaufort. White former slave owners were fleeing by night and asking for help from the slaves whom they had persecuted. Abraham Lincoln was a great President however he had absolutely no intentions of ever freeing any slaves, if it were possible at all to win the war without (1, using no black soldiers) and (2, if it were possible to win the War without freeing any slaves at all! History and the movie industry eagerly tell us how bravely the Negro slave soldiers died at the battle at fort Sumter with actor Denzel Washington and Morgan Freeman, but there is no mention in the media of the heroic emancipation of the slaves in the State of South Carolina in Charleston and Beaufort in 1862, a full year before Abraham Lincoln realized that God was revealing on the battlefield that it was his timing now to set the slaves free! The Southern Confederate Soldiers ran after their defeat at St. Mary's in Charleston and they ran at the battle show of force in Jacksonville Florida. The Confederate Flag is a flag of defeat and it does not have any bearing on me one way or the other, I understand, the confederates still want their slaves back.

Anytime there is a transition of any kind taking place in any land there is always going to be loses that are painful, Our Bible tells us that before the end of time the world will look like a speckled bird meaning that it's people will be of all colors blending into one. After this generation of people who are forty years old and older die out the bigotry and prejudice between the races will cease to exist. Our children who are co-mingling and attending schools together, black, white Mexican and Latino, Asians are all getting along just fine they could care less about what happened in the past with slavery. Within the next fifty years races will become unified, one race. It is difficult to see and acknowledge the changes taking place with only a view from among the crowd on the earth. The only thing that will always remain the same is the wealthy and the poor will be far apart.

My Grandfather told me that his Dad told him that the food that they ate remained the same during slavery as it did during the depression. The people who lived in the Towns and Cities suffered from the shortage of food but on the farms everything remained the same, everyone had gardens and they always kept their seeds for planting from the year before. All animals ate the same also the land provided plenty of food for them but there was no money to buy anything with. He said that during the last months and days of the War the Confederate soldiers were running and hiding in the woods while the slaves were setting fires at night near the hidden camps to alert the Union soldiers of there where a bouts as they escaped. All slaves became spies for the Union soldiers, some slaves traveled as contraband as far as Washington and Baltimore to assist the Union army any way they could. Just like the children of Israel in Egypt were told to go and borrow money, gold and silver to support them on their escape from bondage under the Egyptian rule, the slaves just took the liberty of stealing and taking whatever they wanted or needed for their escape from the long bondage in America. General Rufus Saxton of Beaufort made the decision at Hilton head to commit to the full scale enlistment of the black soldiers because it was key and only way that the Union was going to win the War, the Southern Confederates were defeating the Union even though they had all kinds of modern weaponry and more men in blue uniforms on the ground, the confederates were winning until the black soldier was allowed to fight!

Today there are nineteen black quarterbacks out of fifty nine in the National football league. They are black pitchers in the national baseball league and countless black athletes in both the NBA and the WNBA for women. Venus and Serena Williams own a professional baseball team in Florida. The signs of the change of times has arrived, President Obama will be sworn in for his second term as President of the United States of America in the coming January 2013. Weather white Americans will ever accept the fact that President Obama saved America with his unprecedented bail outs of all of the great powers, the banks and super power Citi-group, the largest insurance company in the world AIG was bailed out and everything in America exist because of the backing of insurance companies. Every time we turn on the TV the news media is trying to supplant doubt and negativism at every hand but they don't understand God's timing has arrived and I've said that "it's time now". There's no way to stop a flowing river and no way to stop the rain from falling, it will certainly be hard for some to accept bu tGod has handpicked Barack Obama to prevent America from falling just like Rome fell!

On Tuesday November 11, 2012 I went to see the movie "Lincoln" produced by Stephen Spielberg, it was a great movie and I would have to admit that I get just as excited about slavery, the Civil War and to see the actual renditions and portrayals of the times of suffering and overcoming as the whites enjoy seeing a rich and extremely prosperous way of life that they lost. I went and had a nice meal at the Golden Coral, my favorite restaurant at one o'clock PM in the afternoon to avoid the large crowds and guest who I saw in the theater at around one thirty? Half full of white senior citizens, no blacks just as I expected. The entire two and a half hour movie was as quiet as they say a church mouse. People my age and above, those of us who remember quiet easily the stories told to us and to see mules and wagons, horses in green pastures. The whites are still trying to figure out what happened to their fortunes and way of life and I'm still trying to see the hand of God move in the plight of over comers in the worst of circumstances. The movie displayed the courage and brilliance of President Lincoln under the very precarious situations, however and understanding the theme was just about Lincoln I was disappointed that there was no mention of the meetings of President Lincoln, Fredrick Douglas and Booker T. Washington, the two most famous and prestigious free black men in America at that time, It was Fredrick Douglas who convinced Lincoln to ultimately send in the one hundred and eighty thousand black volunteer soldiers. Lincoln also hired Harriet Tubman of the Underground Railroad to become a valuable spy for the Union Army. She then recruited numerous spies from all over the South who helped her in the endeavors of bringing slaves to different points of contact and freedom. There were many sail and fishing boats stolen to transport slaves up river by moonlight carrying countless numbers of slaves. The slaves have always been portrayed as stupid victims when actually they were brave and courageous actors and actresses pretending to be absent minded which makes it quite easy to pull the wool over the eyes of the slave masters. Every time that I see footage of the blue and grey Civil War battles and movement it places me directly in the Middle of each battle when I see a black face. It is and unbelievable feeling of excitement of which I cannot begin to explain. I've known for a long time now that anytime a group of people are hoping, praying and waiting for the same identical thing, "Freedom "from pain and suffering, degradation and humiliation it is bound to come to pass. On the other hand while the rich and powerful whites are praying and hoping to keep a people in that kind of condition for all eternity while they are filled with hate for the black race, it completely escapes all of my understanding. God is above looking down at the most powerful people that he created being dehumanized and murdered every day and it is forgotten by the whites before they get back into their wagons to go home and have a drink! There is no ethnicity in America who hates the whites and yet it is the whites who have created words and phrases to belittle every ethnicity in this Country, perhaps that is what power does to you. As I stated earlier we live in a world of opposites, a weak and a strong, a top and a bottom and anytime that you find yourself on the top with nowhere else to go lookout you are someday going to fall. I remember when Mike Tyson compiled thirty seven straight defeats, seven completes you and eight represents the new beginning. One day I hope to produce a movie giving the facts from a black person's point of view, it will be something entirely different, most slaves were never committed to being victims and none were satisfied with their condition, a natural fact.

During the 1920's through the 1970's there was the great migration by blacks from the South to the North to get away from the terrible treatment on blacks by the whites and to create a better way of life. During that time from the early seventies blacks begun migrating back to the South bringing with them their children and Grandchildren who have grown up on the battle fields of life with gang know how and they are not afraid to die. Somehow it seems to have balanced out the aggression of the KKK. I would never suggest a thought of confrontation but it seems to have brought a peace with it. For all races to live in peace would give life a new meaning and that's exactly what God wants for all of his people to live in real peace all over the world. Peace comes when there is no need for anyone to take advantage of another because opportunities for everyone who wants to succeed can do so.

America is the only place on Earth where there is someone from every Nationality living in one Country under the same Government and its laws. There was no America in our Holy Bible but it has become a world power almost from its inception. Rome was the world power but it did not have the diversity in the races competing equally for wealth. Today we have the gang violence from the black race who are continuously killing other blacks, The Mexican and Latino have that very similar problem and then you have the whites and Asians who are committing mass murder at will on innocent victims of all races in publics places without explanation, there's no way to prepare or combat senseless murder. Gang violence is a problem that we all share in the grief of harm to our children and Grandchildren. With the economy being the way that it is with its uncertainty and the hope of finding a good job very bleak, there is no way for our youth and young adults to plan or expect to have a happy and satisfying future. Not only do our seniors have to rear our Grandchildren we have to allow our children to remain in our homes much longer. Having grown children in your home is sometimes not pleasant, not only do they feel the need to respect you they have no fear of you either. Asking them to do something to help out around the house is just like saying, don't bother doing anything I will do it for you;

CHAPTER SEVEN

Seven

The number seven holds many mysteries however it means perfection and completion! The number six means the number for man because God created man on the six day, the number eight means a new beginning, man, completion and a new beginning. Let us take a journey back in time and take a look at some miraculous and powerful beginnings. The number seven cannot be divided by any other number other than itself, and there are seven stages of life, infancy, childhood, adolescents, young adult, adult, elder or senior and old age. There are seven stages of the moon which brings order to nature. When God created Adam he was born a grown Man estimated at age twenty three or twenty four, the age of man's greatest strength in all areas, sexually as well. God brought down a company of his highest ranked Angles, to include the most beautiful and brilliant mind and body, second only to God himself, Satan-Lucifer who had great power, power to change his form into man or animal at will. God brought his Kingdom down to the Earth when he decided to make his most special creation-man; He said let us make man in our own image having a triad (three) components, a soul, spirit and a body. He made Adam in to seven parts which is the number of Devine perfection. Seven parts to the body, the head, neck, torso, two arms and two legs, seven. The blood is seventy five percent water and the Earth is made of seventy five percent water. He took a single blade of running grass and made

Adams hair and a smooth stone he blessed and made his eyes containing as many con cells as it appears the number of stars in the sky seen only under a microscope. These are the foundations that were established, God is the head of man, man is the head of woman, God made man for his glory and he made the woman for man' glory—but woman's glory is her crown(her hair) and woman was not made from the grown but from the side of man, his rib. Let us establish here that the woman Eve never had a chance against Satan, he was too magnificent, beautiful because he was a man when she met him and only turned into a snake when God cursed him, however he has the power to change himself out of that form. Eve was never given the laws of God only Adam received them and that is the reason they both were punished; Plato expounded on some of the above in" Devine Harmony". According to medical science the human body contains more cells than the universe has stars. Man has sixty thousand miles of blood vessels and the human eye has one hundred and twenty million rod cells and seven million con cells. God blessed Adam and made his head holy unto him, he left seven openings in Adams head, two eyes, two ears, two nostrils and the mouth, a mouth which has the capability of creating things from words spoken, man can speak life or death with his mouth so the mouth should be kept clean for holy utterances;

The eye can process colors and information faster than any super computer imagined in the future creations. Every seven days the human body replaces all cells contained within the body and when one cell dies and divides, two hundred cells are reproduced. We are constantly dropping and shedding cells from our bodies and that is the reason that a blood hound can track you anywhere except through water. Now, let's take look into Adam's garden as extensive research reveals.

On the six day of God's creation after great thought and preparation of the Earth, He placed gold, silver, uranium and all kinds of oils. All trees, flowers fruits and vegetables, everything was perfect including the normal temperature of seventy degrees. God brought his kingdom down and connected the heaven to the Earth, thy kingdom come on Earth just as it is in heaven. He took a stone and divided it into the seven parts which I just mentioned. He constructed a perfect twenty seven bones in each hand so that Adam could work, play, and cuddle his wife and tiny infant child. Man thinks as we all have been taught that righteous living is holy unto God but we do not think like God, he left the seven openings which is holy unto him and when only he is ready he changes our behavior. Connecting heaven to the Earth is sententious speaking in that he connects the invisible world of spirit to the physical world. God made Adam's heart last and he constructed an invisible round container in which he placed the invisible heaven and earth so that anytime Adam thought about God's kingdom, it was in his heart and the more he thought about the kingdom it would expand, along with his thoughts. Anytime that we think about anything it expands, trouble, obstacles as well as love, it expands. When God breathed into Adam's nostrils the breath of life and awakened him and took a long walk through the garden showing him all of the other creations, as Adam walked with God hovering over him in a cloud he realized that he could see through the sky into the seventh heaven, where God's feet rest. He told Adam to look out over the waters as he explained that he had made seven oceans and seven major seas. He explained to Adam the world was made of the laws of opposites which is a balance of universal order, there is a night and day, a high and a low, a wet and a dry, a sunset and a sunrise, a warm and a cold, there is life and death Adam but you shall live forever if you follow my instructions. There are seven churches and seven spirits of God, there is happiness always followed by sadness. Happiness is the most precious thing that we can hope for and that is why I'm always looking for something or someone who can bring me an excitement to look forward to. Anytime sadness or obstacles show up in my life I simply close my eyes momentarily and say to myself, "this is just temporary".

There are numerous volumes of lost books of the bible which intrigue and fascinate me greatly. Through ON TTRACC BIBLE BUSINESS COLLEGE I often request and receive information from several Universities around the world to include the University of Jerusalem. In the "forgotten books of Eden" Adam could have lived one or two hundred years in the garden being taught and learning the precepts of God's universal thinking in which he conveyed to Adam the purpose of life long term, for eternity and beyond. Understanding that there was no youth and adolescence to focus on-Adam was born without having to ever experience the pressures and growing pains that we all have to endure. Once when I was meditating and floating upwards towards heaven I heard the profound voice that I was familiar with from my childhood say to me "Arvanie" my middle name, if you don't go back now, what will your life mean to the world and to the glory of God? What have you done with your creative power? The wise geniuses of old teaches us that God thinks on a universal scale and selects individuals whom he has sent into the world at various times chronologically to do and solve certain world problems during the era and times that we live in. My mind was directed to my dream immediately, to build businesses to help solve the problem of unemployment in my State and most of all my home town Marion County in the Pee Dee. Adam's purpose was to develop the garden into a metropolis, build cities and buildings along with the agricultural venue to accommodate the human population that God was going to send through Adam's genealogy and his seed. Adam possessed in his body the genealogy of every nationality on earth today, all blacks, whites, Chinese, Japanese and Indian races in the universe over a period of time that would never be measured by years or centuries. Archeologist, Historians and Evolutionist are limiting and basing their thoughts and ideas on the premise that we are the second generations of people who have populated the earth when God has always been-always existed and he has populated his earth many times. In the book of Geneses from the beginning God said "let us make man to replenish the earth, replenish! Adam was alone having seen no woman or other human before Eve but he had wisdom from God and no one ever uses wisdom correctly before the age of thirty as Jesus demonstrated by only beginning his ministry at age thirty. At night after work Adam used his time thinking and hoping, meditating and dreaming, he had complete dominion over the entire earth but was only supposed to branch out over other lands after he completed his work in the Garden of Eden. Adam could call any animal, Lion Tiger, deer or elk and they would just come to him and humbly lie die and be slain if it was Adam's desire. There was no pesky weeds and the insects would obey Adam's voice when he command them to flee from his vegetation. There were four rivers flowing beautifully through the garden which brought nutrients to nourish his fields and seafood of all kinds, all rivers run into the ocean of salt water making a path of fresh water at the bottom and never mix. Salt water fish is taken from the sea but one has to apply salt to the fish before you can eat them, miraculous! The ocean floor turns upside down in various places and washed all kinds of fish and other seafood out onto the seashore for Adam to eat without having to catch them. Fruit trees gave of their fruit in abundance all during the year without cold weather to freeze them.

In Defense of Eve

I'm dedicating this as a result of my investigative report as I viewed the trespassing of the Uninvited guest in the beautiful Garden of Eden that God created for Adam and his bride. There is no mistake in the molecular structure of Man and his definitive need to visually see and interpret the beauty of a woman. The Taj mahal in India is a representation of the love of a man for his woman and so is the destruction of Gaza by Samson and the Philistines after the King tricked his bride to be into revealing the secret of his riddle at his bridegroom party. Eve was created and designed especially for Adam and his preferences in the face and body, curves and hips legs and feet of a woman. As he waved goodbye to his beautiful bride as he left for the work of tending to his Garden, he had no clue as to what was about to happen to his world. Eve was bathing in a nearby river after she had prepared breakfast and saw her husband walk away in his nakedness as they both were accustomed to, she dried herself off and began to comb her long black thick wavy and bushy hair. Suddenly she looked into the shade of a tree with beautiful blossoms with a fragrance of honey suckle and rose with lemon combined and there stood a tall and the most beautifully handsome man just leaning against the tree wearing a beautiful powder blue suit, navy blue and white shoes, a bright silk yellow tie with a matching lapel handkerchief. He sported a long Gold chain through the vest in front of his waist and a wide bream faun colored hat with blue feathers in the left side of his hat. Eve was caramel colored and naked as this man-Satan looked upon her as if he simply adored her from afar, looking deep into her eyes.

Satan was formally the most beautiful, wise and the most powerful and highest ranking Angel in God's Kingdom. God created him with the ability to change his form -at will allowing him to challenge any creature on the Earth. During God's creation of Adam, when he was finished God told all of his Angels present to" bow down to Adam, when Satan rebelled "and refused to do so saying that he had been created millenniums before Adam and that he could trick him any time he chose to. God Kicked Satan out of heaven with his persuasive and trickiness with a free hand to confuse or tamper with anyone he chose to, he is a spirit and can never die so he does just what he wants to with limits until God says "it's time now". Satan began talking to Eve with a smooth silky voice and his ability to romance any woman with his charismatic flow of speech. Eve never had a chance as no one would have, Satan is from the spirit world which is beyond the human capacity to comprehend fully. Satan told Eve that he just happened to bring her a silk semi see through gown, pinkish with a red rosy design and low cut breast line. As he put his arm around her and begun to tell her some of the things that he could do to her to make her feel total bliss, let us talk-talk and pillow talk. Eve was happy and greatly impressed so as they laid down together and he gave her the fruit she was literally in another world. The silky gown felt smooth on her skin and the pinkish color was completely new to her.

There have been times when I was romancing a beautiful woman by candle light over some cocktails and listening to soft music, it truly made no difference what her mom told her over her lifetime about first dates, I could convince her if I said something like "how can this be forbidden, if it's "love". Woman has a uniqueness and the intrinsic intuition that no man can explain or understand, she can since danger under uncommon circumstances. Woman carries an unborn child underneath her heart for nine months and gives all of her complete love to that child and she will never turn her back on the child under normal circumstances, consequently the child never wants to leave the place where it is always experiencing the love of its mom.

When Adam and Eve got kicked out of the perfect Garden he was heartbroken and Eve was deeply saddened for him. Nothing would grow for food as it had in the Garden, the weeds overtook everything that he planted and he had to make different types of fish for fertilizer whereas that was not necessary in the Garden. He missed the long walks talking to God everyday about any and every thing. He couldn't see beyond the sky anymore and all of the animals became afraid of him and ran when they saw or smelled him. He had to learn how to fish and work every day for his food. Sadly he tried unsuccessfully to get back into the Garden but two large Angels were guarding the entrance. Adam tried to drown himself but it was Eve who saved him, he tried to starve himself to death by hiding in a cave but it was Eve who found him and saved him twice. He tried to throw himself down off a cliff twice but the Angels caught him and saved him. It has been easy to lay all blame on Eve for getting Adam kicked out of the Garden but in retrospect it would have happened to any woman and perhaps man as well if he caught Adam at a weak moment; It is difficult to understand, God knew that Satan would go through Eve to get to Adam however he expected Adam to stand up, rebuke his wife and counsel her sternly and teach her the rules of the land. God expects men to stand up and lead his wife and family, if it were such that man could earn enough money so that his wife has the choice to work or not to, and after the childrearing years to start her own business if she chooses, there would be a lot less stress on a marriage. Women has enhanced the work force but at a high cost in some cases however I do believe in equality on that matter, God has given woman the ability to do great things and I'm proud for them. There would be no Church to speak of or schools balanced for the measure of teaching and learning. Women have a tremendous amount of patience and persuasive ability that man simply do not have. I think that women look better longer if she has a career and more opportunity to use her intuitive skills. The work place is not about muscular activities any longer it is about thinking and adjusting to different ways to do different things. I actually enjoy women's basketball more than I do the NBA where everything is about being tall, players don't get to use the unique physical abilities that they have anymore. It has always been such that too many men go to war and die or become disable to some degree and women have to become both parents.

Jesus Birth

When I was seven years old and in the third grade I was portraying the part of the black King who gave Jesus the gold at his birth. As I was standing in the candle light on stage watching the other two class mates who were the other two Kings give their gifts to the young girl who played Mary, the mother of Jesus I had a serious optical illusion, everyone on stage were black and we were giving gifts to the baby Jesus who was a "white doll", it was disturbing to me and it has caused me great concern until I became an adult out of College during research and studying metaphysics. Anyone will tell you who has ever been to the Holy Land as everyone in Jerusalem knows that the Christmas story of Jesus being born in stable with animals standing around is a myth! I found out for myself (lost books of Eden) and several other sources comply as well, God planned and arraigned the entire circumstances and events surrounding the birth of the only "son of God in whom he loves and is well pleased" since the event of Satan beguiling Eve both she and Adam sinned.

Let's see if your teacher will appear at this moment; Two years before Jesus birth God sent two Angels to the edge of the city of Jerusalem through the desert edge where hills and mountains were standing as cover for a hiding place and commanded the Angels to hue out a dwelling place for a home in a huge rock, just like the burial rocks are hewn out today. God commanded a star to shine three times brighter than any other stars in the sky in the Eastern parts of the Middle east to attract the attention of three wise and rich kings that he selected and spoke the words of the birth of the new born King two years in advance because the Kings were the sons of "Ham, Shem and Japheth" and it would take two years for them to meet and take the journey together. Each King travels by caravan totaling at least two hundred guards and servants for the King's protection with his wealth. After the star led them to King Herod's palace the Kings met with Herod and discussed the purpose for their journey into Jerusalem with all of the companies of guards and servants to advise him that they meant him no harm, just a visit to a new born King. Meanwhile as Joseph and Mary were approaching the entrance of the cave that was prepared for them, the unborn fetus in Mary's womb began to press hard against her stomach, so hard until she couldn't go on, Joseph saw the light from the star shinning on the entrance of the cave and he took Mary down from the donkey and took her inside the cave. Mary was in extreme pain and she told Joseph to hurry and get a midwife for her delivery. Joseph began running towards the City of Jerusalem but there was an old lady already walking towards the cave entrance. Before he could turn around and go back, there was a tremendous crowd of people hurrying towards him talking with great excitement because they saw the bright star shinning but they didn't know what to expect, Joseph just fell down on his face for fear that they were coming to kill him or to bring harm to him as a stranger in the land. It seems that if by coincidence, perhaps, but i don't think so, this old woman had been a prostitute in her young life but now she worked in the employ of her brother who was a druggist. This woman got a pale of water from a nearby stream and went inside to deliver Jesus, she saw a blinding light coming from the womb of Mary and she was startled that the miracle birth of Jesus had no umbilical card to cut. The light surrounding Jesus was brighter than the star had ever been over the two year period. She took the baby Jesus and washed him clean and Jesus opened his eyes and looked at her until she went into a trance, the power emanating from the baby Jesus came upon the old woman and blessed her and restored her back to her youth, she became the same age as Mary, fourteen years of age, her name was Mary Magdalene! The two angels appeared at the entrance of the cave and told her that she had received the first blessing of the new King of Kings, Jesus the Christ. As Joseph made his way back through the crowd and held the new born baby, Mary Magdalene, the midwife took the bath water that she had bathed Jesus in and walked backwards towards the cave entrance as she was so completely fascinated that she couldn't take her eyes off Jesus, she threw the bath water over her shoulder out into the crowd and every drop and even the mist from the water that landed on the people who were sick, crippled or deaf, they were all healed in an instant. After the three Kings were allowed to come in they gave Jesus enough gold, silver, Mur and incents to support and provide all living expenses for travel accommodations for the trip and settling funds for the entire family for two years and longer. The Kings told Joseph that King Herod would be looking for the baby Jesus as he asked them to return to him with the news of where Jesus was, he wanted to kill Jesus so the three Kings left town on a different route. They told Joseph that there was a stable for animals in Jerusalem that they had already arraigned and paid for which would be a perfect place for hiding until the eighth day, which would be the day for Jesus circumcision, the Jewish custom. On the eighth day at Jesus ceremony to be circumcised Mary Magdalene asked for the foreskin of Jesus which she kept in a solution from her brother's drug store, she kept it in an" alabaster box" until the day at Lazarus house when she applied it to the feet and head of Jesus seven days before Jesus was crucified. Immediately following the ceremony Joseph took Jesus and Mary on the Journey to Egypt where they lived for two years until King "Herod's" death.

After I had the spontaneous mental illusion on the stage the night that I became a rich King from Africa with enough Gold to give to the King of Kings freely with love and respect without any concerns, it changed my thinking forever. When I was at home playing with my younger brother it became my total responsibility to love and protect my brother at all and any cost. As soon as he went to sleep for an afternoon nap I slipped out of the house, took our dog Brownie and I was off, into the fields and down the dirt road analyzing my new territory. I went into the woods and found the perfect spot for my camp that no one could find, in a clearing surrounded by bushy trees with low hanging branches that I could climb up on quickly to see if anyone was ever approaching to close to my camp I could swing from tree branch to branch to throw them off. Sitting and lying down just daydreaming was the perfect relaxation and most fascinating way to travel in my mind in the forest with the cool breezes and birds chirping close to me without moving, they never knew that I was there. Brownie would go away by himself which left me alone exactly as I liked it, so that I could commune with nature and create a world for myself and my family when I got older, richer and wiser. I often thought about each person in my class and decide what they would be doing as adults, what kind of work would they do? As for me I would be working in my office in a big beautiful building in a large City. My little brother was born with a profound and distinctive temper and the things that he wanted to do was to follow me when he could. When I often came home and he didn't know where I had been he knew that I was doing something that was fun and he didn't like the idea that he had missed it so he would fuss at mom for not awakening him so that he could go. That fussing always got him in a lot of trouble but he did not care, if mom or Dad started to spank or whip my brother DG, "great day" he would fall down on the floor and take a deep breath, and 'hold it", and hold it, and hold it until he was about to pass out! Mom would pick him up and run with him, shaking him to get him to come back to life but it didn't matter, the only way that DG would take in a breath of air was if mom placed him in my lap and he heard my voice, calling, DG come on now, come on. After woods I would just look at him and say to myself, gait day boy you were willing to kill yourself for your strong constitutional beliefs. DG is that same way today about his work, no one can match his work ethic he is simply tenacious, if someone or a supervisor tries to set road blocks to prevent him from being successful-the most successful in the entire agency and departments, he simply goes into his world until he finds the answer, he has absolutely no rivals when it comes to his management skills. I was extremely excited when I found the information concerning the end of Jesus two year stay in Egypt after King Herod's death.

On the road leading out of the city of Egypt where merchants and business people came in and out of the city, there was always young boys in age ranges from thirteen through nineteen or so just hanging out at the edge of the city to rob and pillage the business men after they had sold their livestock and other products. Almost like the young gang activity that exist in many cities today, young men who do not work want to capitalize on the wealth of others except today the product is drugs. When Joseph reached the outer gates of Egypt the young gang members approached him and asked him to hand over all monies, to include camels, goats and gold. Jesus was only two years old in his mother's arms riding on the donkey when he leaned upward and looked at the two gang leaders and said sternly, your fathers father- he went back one thousand years into the boys family histories and told them some of the stories that had been passed down to them for generations and quiet equivocally if you young boys do not change your ways and live better, within thirty years you will both wind up hanging from a tree. One of the boys whose name was Titus, as they both were trembling, went and brought forty goats of his own and gave them to Jesus, the other boy's name was Dumachuss, I call him dumb ass, just shirked with anger and walked away. These were the same two men who wound up on the cross with Jesus thirty years later and the one on Jesus left was the one who recognized Jesus and asked him to remember me when you get into your "Kingdom", the other was the one who said the dumb words, If you are such a king why don't you get yourself free and down from here? Titus was saved on the cross that day and the only good thing that he had ever done was to respect Jesus and to give him the forty goats. The seeds that you plant each day of your life are the good fruits that you will harvest tomorrow.

My brother DG taught me a powerful lesson concerning non-violence long before we ever heard of Dr. Martin L. King Jr. in the 60's, for instance the essence of nonviolence is designed to bring about change from within the people who are discriminating against you. In the mid-fifties when I was around eight years old and DG was six we had a bicycle together, one that we got for Christmas which had the training wheels on it for my little brother who couldn't catch on to riding without the wheels as quickly as I did. You see, taking the training wheels off and putting them back on just so that my brother could ride quickly became too cumbersome for me, I was quick to learn and off and gone. One day my friend Lee and I were riding, racing and just playing around when my brother kept asking me to take the wheels off so that he could ride, it was his turn, well Lee suggested that we ride up on hwy.

501 a good distance, too far for DG to follow. We rode about two miles way up 501 hwy. and looked back and wouldn't you know that my brother was coming as fast as he could and crying to boot! When he got to where we were he didn't say a word, just sniffling with tears running down his face. I said DG go back home now! He didn't say anything so I punched him in his chest-hard go home boy! This kid knew that he couldn't beat me so his anger heightened-escalated, he squared his shoulders and took a step closer such that he was inviting me to hit him again at will, take your best shot again and crying harder at the same time. I looked into his eyes and I knew that he was never going to give up, half of the bike was his and it was his turn to ride, plain and simple he wasn't going to go away. Whatever countenance that I had-fell and my guilt along with it. I stop listening to Lee and pushed the bike all of the way back until we got safely back into Rains and gave him the bicycle so that he could ride with

the training wheels put back on and guest what? What ED? I went into the woods into my camp alone, told Lee to go home and I cried from the guilt of not only keeping my little brother whom I loved from riding his turn but hitting him in his chest from my own selfishness to boot! That's when I found out what nonviolence was all about so when I heard about it years later with the civil rights movement I knew that it was a winner even though someone would surely have to suffer. Today my brother works for the Federal Government however he used to work for a State Agency as I did and there was always someone who thought that they could do your job as good or better than you could and at the same time the higher ups, supervisors created secret obstacles to prevent you from successfully doing the duties pertaining to your job. There was always the obstacle placed in your path that would allow supervisors to give you an unsatisfactory evaluation and consequently demote you in order to give your job to a friend or associate that they wanted to give your job to. I quit, I wanted to think about things other than the people on my job, Mutual of Omaha gave me that freedom however my brother DG would rather fight than switch, he would examine the alternatives from all stand points with an understanding of the outcome on either hand and coming from either direction six months in advance so that when they dropped and obstacle on the table, he would simply reach into his briefcase and pull out a typed referendum which applies directly to the subject matter at hand accompanied with a complete and viable solution to the problem that his supervisors were getting ready to introduce to trap him and bring about a road block for him which would need attention in one week, they thought that there would be no possible way to complete the task however my brother not only had the answer, he had the answer to the next ambiguous problem that they could think up within the next two years. My brother has an impeccable work ethic which is un-rivaled in the field that he is in and refuses to be beaten.

When Jesus went to his good friend Lazarus tomb the timing was precisely seven days before he was to be crucified, and Lazarus house was exactly seven miles from Jericho where he went and made his famous pit stop to heal the blind man who had been waiting for Jesus since the night that King Herod gave the order to kill every child two years old and under trying to kill Jesus, the King of Kings. This man remembered the alabaster box and he heard about the woman who used the expensive smelling perfume to apply it to the head and feet of Jesus in the home of Lazarus, Mary Magdalene. I have no adverse thoughts about any woman in the Bible days who had to subject themselves to prostitution in order to feed and support themselves. If a woman had no husband or no male child it was impossible for them to own land or any property to provide a stable living for themselves and the men of those days thought, it unworthy to live past the age of thirty when it was of the highest honor to give their lives for country and to die for their King. Mary Magdalene had a very special relationship with Jesus, she was there as one of the only three witnesses of his miracle birth, the other two were Angels.

Pontius Eurelius Pilate—No Coward

As a young boy during Easter Sunday services was a big deal in Rains, my home. But year after year I was confused at so many preachers main topic in their message was that of the Governor of Jerusalem, Pontius Pilate was portrayed as a common coward! I was deeply bothered by that idea because I had great admiration and respect for preachers however I had ideas and a completely different understanding of the actions of Pilate at the trial of Jesus Christ. First of all let's take a look at the life and journey of" Pontius Eurelius Pilate".

Pilate was born in Rome the son of King Herod, born of Royal blood but his problem was as many other children of that era, he was only the son of Herod's six wife- born in a harem, which afforded him absolutely no fame, inheritance or status. When the young Pilate reached the age of sixteen he was very ambitious and determined to gain both fame and fortune because he wanted to be a Caesar being that his father was of Royal blood and he grew up around rich kids in the palace. He joined the military Roman forces and progressed well in his training. Pilate was ambidextrous, he could yield a sword with both hands equally and one day while he was practicing he accidentally killed a soldier who was training him and he had to flee into Caesarea until he reached the age of twenty. At the age of twenty he had surpassed all army personnel in his legion. He had fallen in love with a young maiden Named Procla, who was the daughter of Tiberius-here again she was born of Tiberius third wife and no inherited rights. Pilate received the promotion and the title of Procurator of Jerusalem so he married Procla and began the Journey to Jerusalem with one thousand foot soldiers under his command and his wife in whom he loved and trusted. When Pilate reached the city gates of Jerusalem he didn't see any idol Gods as he was accustomed to in Rome almost on every corner so he sent one hundred and twenty of his soldiers back to Rome before he entered the city to bring back the Idol Gods "Bail "and the idol God" Dagon". He knew that the Jews were powerful and he wanted familiar Gods in his presence before he entered the Holy city of Jerusalem. There is nothing under the sun that is of any significance that happens without God; When the decision was made in God's Kingdom to send his only son Jesus into the world to redeem man and save him from sin, he started at the end of his life by sending Pontius Eurelius "Pilate", to end the way of Jesus by taking his very life! Pilate was only one year older than Jesus, He sent his first cousin "John" to prepare his way, and six months later he sent the Christ Jesus who was the "way" the truth and the life! Prior to Pilate getting the promotion to go to Jerusalem as the third Procurator two others had already gone to assume the title however they got kicked out by the powerful Jews within less than three years. Pilate was Procurator in Jerusalem for eleven years by the time he came in contact with Jesus. Pilate was treacherous; he had been tested and proven many times on the battle field and he made his name into greatness as a famous warrior, he was fearless. He kept his foot on the necks of the Jews by confiscating their rich treasury, he kept their ceremonial robes and they were not allowed to conduct parades without the strict permission of Pilate. As procurator he had total control of all life in the jurisdiction of Jerusalem, meaning that there could be no sacrifices of dead animals as offerings, not even a dove could be killed without Pilate's permission! Now then, let's go into the business of conducting the trial of Jesus Christ. The night before the Trial of Jesus, Pilate's wife Procla who seems to have always had severe headaches, Migraine headaches from my best understanding, she stayed in the bedroom almost all of the time,

She and Pilate never had any children. Procla was lying down when suddenly, without any warning the Holy Spirit came into the bedroom and touched her on the forehead, and she was healed instantly. The Holy Spirit told her to tell her husband Pilate to do exactly what Jesus tells him to do on tomorrow, Jesus is the true and only son of God and he was sent into the world to die for the sins of the entire world, and as the Spirit left she began to shout Holy praises to the Lord. In the meantime Pilate was in Court giving the order for Jesus to be whipped, flogged thirty nine lashes with the whip that was called "the cat of nine tails", a leather strap which is constructed with the implementation of nine different types of bone, tacks and other metal objects which was designed to cut and tear the flesh open on contact. Procla had visited one of Jesus sermons on the steps of the temple in the city of Jerusalem and told Pilate beforehand to have nothing to do with Jesus, there was something about him that both worried and pleased her at the same time. When Pilate walked out of the headquarters court room and down the halls toward his living quarters he heard Procla, his wife screaming and shouting praising the Lord she had not only been healed she had received the Holy Spirit as well. Pilate opened the door to his bedroom and Procla leaped into his arms telling him that the man that you just ordered to be whipped is the true son of God; He realized quickly that she had been healed of the headaches because she had never acted with such excitement before in her life. After she finished telling him the full details Pilate just commenced to walk the floor, he had felt an uneasiness all of the time that he was talking to Jesus and he could not settle on just what it was. He remembered everything that Jesus had told him that he had no power to do anything to him unless he received it from his father in Heaven above. Pilate was unable to sleep that night he just walked the floor until daybreak and there was a knock at his door. The military officer told Pilate that the prisoner was ready and that it would be best if he finished sentencing Jesus because he was almost dead, two thirds dead from the vicious flesh tearing whipping he had received. Pilate looked over at his wife and she was constantly shaking her head, no, do not do anything else to Jesus he is the son of the almighty God; So he walked out and took his seat in the Judges seat, He pondered and looked out into the crowd at the hate he saw on the faces of the people in the crowd, Satan had dispatched his evil Angels throughout the crowd and they were saying "kill him, kill Jesus" and they were threatening to stab and cut anyone who said otherwise!

Pilate had intended for the thirty nine lashes to be for Jesus bail and he could set him free without further concerns but the crowd was out of control, he couldn't even exercise the Jewish holiday choice of setting Barabbas or Jesus free so he called Jesus over to him to talk and counsel him, ask him who are you? Where did you come from? Are you a King? Jesus was standing in a pool of his own blood and as he began to take short steps towards Pilate the two Idol Gods which was standing in the hallway on either side, the God Bail and Idol God Dagon which was made of wood and cement began to real and rock back and forth as if they were trying to bow down to Jesus, the King of Kings. Pilate and the Pharisees saw it and Pilate ordered Jesus to go back and walk back through again they thought that someone was playing a trick somehow. When Jesus began to walk again a stream of his blood started to flow in front of Jesus and this time the idol Gods both fell down and crashed, a strong wind just blew them both away into the dust. When a single drop of Jesus blood found its way into a crack in the cement floor it went down to the water table underneath the ground and caused the earth to tremble, earthquakes began to erupt all over the world, all of the animals in the fields and pastures were bowing their heads down but not one could take a drink of water at the trawfts and streams. Rocks began to break open in the mountains, I guest this was what all of the preachers were talking about when they said that Pilate was a coward. Pilate walked up to Jesus and told him that he was going to set him free if he wanted him to but Jesus told him to hurry, for this is what I came into the world for. Pilate washed his hands of the matter in public and said I see no fault in this man; it is of your own doing to murder this man and it will be on the heads of your children's children. As the soldiers were taking Jesus up to Golgotha to hang him from the cross some of the people saw men who had been dead for five hundred years and longer. When Jesus was hanging from the cross his mother Mary, Mary of Magdala and Mary Magdalene but his mother Mary was crying as to suffer herself unto death and to go home with her son Jesus. Jesus spoke seven times from the cross and on his seventh and final saying God opened up the Heavens so that Mary saw the prepared robe with bright golden sash and his Angels were all beckoning him to come on home, Mary was pleased and began singing as she led the people down from the hill. Titus was saved that day as Jesus told him, this day you will be with me in paradise. The power which was emanating from Jesus body caused heavy and adverse reactions in the universe all over the world, earthquakes erupted and swallowed up all of the people that was in the crowd saying kill Jesus, let's crucify him, the sun hung down low and refused to shine, the moon hung low dripping blood. The soldiers who took Jesus clothing and placed them in the fire quickly realized that none of them would burn so they gambled with dice for his robe and other clothing. Today we simply consider the day that Jesus died on the cross to save all mankind from sin forever as just good Friday, you must consider the fact that the creator of the entire universe freely gave his life for his children. The instant that Jesus gave up the Ghost, everything in the heavens erupted, the lightning flashed across the dark and dreary skies all over the world, not just on the hill of Golgotha, the sun that God created refused to shine for the entire three hours that Jesus hung on the cross, it rained immediately after the Centurion soldier stabbed Jesus in his side and blood and water flowed down his body and touched the ground, it opened up and the water from underneath the earth gushed upward and flowed all over and through the streets of Jerusalem washing away sin from the city. Jesus spirit immediately went into Heaven where he placed a drop of his blood on the mercy seat to bind sin both in heaven and in the earth.

Julius Cesar had contracted an illness which from the description to me seemed to be diabetes and diverticulitis, his wife had a sleeping sickness where she fell to sleep anywhere and anytime, even while sitting down to a table at mealtimes. Cesar sent a rider on horseback which was the normal carrier from Rome to Jerusalem to tell Pontius Pilate to send Jesus to heal him and his wife as he had heard that Jesus could heal you without touching you and from afar as well as witnessed by all after the Centurion asked Jesus to heal his servant, knowing that all Jesus had to do was just say the word and he would be healed. It was too late, Pilate had hung Jesus the day before and Pilate feared for his life because he knew that the penalty for disobeying a direct order from the Emperor was death by beheading and a dishonorable death, Pilate went out on his back balcony and fell on his sword, he committed suicide. Jesus hung on the cross from the six to the ninth hour, 1: pm in the afternoon until 3:pm. The apostle John whom Jesus told and designated as to become the son of his mother Mary at the cross took her to Ephesus a few months after the day of Jubilee and built a house for her which still stands today.

Samson and the love of "his woman"

Over the years many people have told me that the information which is not written in our Holy Bible, they are not interested in knowing it when it comes to theology. I have read my Bible nine times and scanned it twice and found several fragments and phrases which appear to have been interjected spontaneously to prompt and provoke serious thought and research. I know that our Holy Bible has been changed seven times, not to mention all of the books that did not make the cut when the canonization process was taking place. Our present King James Version translated in 1511 was done by fifty scribes hired and commissioned by King James. A scribe is an individual who has been trained from early childhood to write perfectly with a beautiful hand writing from the right side of the page to the left we write from left to right. A calligrapher is a local trained professional writer which was hired to do the same written documentation but hired by the public and Roman Government, scribes were employed by the Pharisees and Sadducees of the Sanhedrin therefore a whole lot of information has been left out of our Bibles, however there is more than enough information therein for the normal average reader.

Abraham is the Father of Isaac and Isaac is the father of Esau and Jacob, the twin boys whom God sent into the world to represent two distinct Nations of people, Esau is to represent the African Nation and Jacob is to represent the White Nation of people. The Bible says that out of Esau twelve Princes would be born and out of Jacob twelve Kings as well and they both would be blessed. Jacob had six sons by his first wife Leah, then four sons by his concubines and by the wife that he truly loved Rachel would be born Joseph and Benjamin. The four sons by the concubines became listed in our Bible as the Judges! Is-sachar, Dan, Naphtali and Gad. The Tribe of Dan was given the land just below Somalia South of Ethiopia by Jacob and today many of the inhabitants wear dreads in their hair, seven braded dread Locks were cut from Samson's head during his encounter and courtship of the infamous "Delilah" however this story is not about Delilah this is about a beautiful young woman that Samson met and fell deeply in love with at the age of twenty and was engaged to be married. As I alluded to earlier in this book, there is nothing of any significance that happens in life without God. There was an old woman in the tribe of Dan- her husband's name was Ma-Noah, she was way past her child bearing years so she prayed and nothing happened. The Philistines were constantly overtaking the Danites, destroying crops after taking whatever they wanted, raping the women and killing off the men who resisted. One day when it was in God's timing he sent an Angel to Hanna in the field and told her that she would bear a son and he was to be raised and cared for as a Nazarene, Samson was a Nazarite. No razor was to ever touch his head and he was to never touch or handle any dead thing and to never have strong drink! Adam, Samson and Jesus were by God and their heads were Holy unto him. Samson met a woman in Tim-nath, a city within the Philistine Territory and fell deeply in love. All of the women in Samson's tribe were bush dwellers in the country side and they used animal fat on their skin to keep it moist and other wild smelly mixtures in their hair. The young woman in the city wore beautiful clothes and used sweet smelling fragrances on her skin and hair. God used this mechanism to lure and raise his Holy spirit up in Samson in order to create friction with the Philistines. Samson saw this woman one day in (my imagination) the open fruit and vegetable market with her sister shopping, about 36-24-36 hips. she had caramel colored skin and long black wavy hair, he walked up to her and took her by the waist and picked her up above his head, as I used to do in Baltimore, and said you're such a beautiful girl, is there any reason why you shouldn't be mine? She said maybe not, who are you? I'm the mighty Samson the only true "Bull of the woods", there is no one like Samson! They walked and talked by the hanging gardens above the beautiful lake with swans swimming and blue jays playing in the springtime. Sometime past and they were in love and decided to be married. As Samson was on his way to the city of Gaza a Lion leaped out and attacked him but the spirit of God rose up in Samson and he slew the lion with his bare hands. The scripture said that Samson tore the lion cross ways, one hand in the top of his mouth and the other hand in the bottom and he pulled with great might and tore the lion in two halves. The flesh of the lion decayed and the honey bees went inside of him and made a hive and honey. Samson took some of the honey and ate it, he carried some home and gave it to his mother without telling her that he had taken it from the carcass of a dead lion. Two of his laws were broken in this one act, the only one left was the taking of strong drink which he didn't deliberately do for over ten years later. Samson had been seen doing some powerful feats unto the Philistines and they were determined to nail him. The day of Samson's engagement party came and as customary it lasted for seven days however on the first day of the party Samson told a riddle to the Philistine guest which included the King of the Philistines, Samson's bride to be was the daughter of a wealthy businessman so some very influential people were at the party. He said out of the eater came something sweeter, what am i? None of the quest could answer the riddle and there was a wager of thirty garments of clothing and thirty sheets. The Philistine King was not only angry he was jealous as well; He took the bride to be and her father into the house about mid-week and told her that if she didn't find the answer to the riddle and tell him he was going to burn her and her father's house down with them inside. She begged and pleaded with Samson to tell her the answer to the riddle and even though she knew Samson's might and fame, she was afraid for her beloved father. Samson finally gave in to her and told her the answer, the King used the infidelity by his bride to embarrass Samson in front of all the guest, Samson's anger rose up within him and he walked into the city of Gaza at a gathering of several of the King's soldiers and slew them hip and thigh, took off their clothing and carried them back to the party and threw them in the king's face. Needless to say Kings do not take lightly to commoners embarrassing them so he ordered one thousand of his soldiers to track Samson down and bring him in chained and bound. The soldiers didn't realize until the next morning when they mounted up to go and capture Samson, in his anger the night before he left the city, snatched the gates of the city off and pulled the stabilizing post up out of the ground and carried them up high on top of a high mountain where only mountain goats could go. The gates weighted two tons each- four thousand pounds, the stabilizing posts weighted four tons each for a total of sixteen thousand pounds that he carried off and up on top of the mountain! God was deliberately kindling the anger of Mighty Samson! He returned to his father in-laws house a week later to pick up his bride but his father in law gave Samson's wife to his best friend by order of the King. God Kindled the spirit of anger in Samson even higher and he tied fire sticks (firebrands) to the tails of foxes and turned them all three hundred loose into the corn and wheat fields of the philistines. Not only did Samson feel betrayed by his wife he was deadly serious about what to do to the King, his wife in bed with his best friend from childhood. All of Samson's life he had often dreamed of the Jawbone of an ass and the two great pillars supporting the huge stadium where all banquets of the King had his invited Kings and other guest to party often. When the soldiers caught up with Samson he was waiting for them by the brook where he spotted the Jawbone of the ass. When they started to cross the brook to take Samson into custody he picked up the jawbone and commenced to swinging. Samson killed another thousand soldiers that day, there was absolutely nothing that the philistines could do with Samson until ten years later when he was thirty" seven "years old, he felt entitled so he began drinking and seducing women at will. This gives me the opportunity to express the realism in the fact that all love comes from God, he sends it to whom he will in different phases and no one is supposed to be able to successfully keep your first "love". When two people fall in love for the first time it is designed to be a learning experience of the pain of being hurt by love. Love is the "only" thing that God "needs" from humans. Two people in love for the first will grow to become too great, nothing can stop that kind of love from getting in between God, Man and woman.

Once when I was In Baltimore living with my brother Billy G. for a summer and he had just bought a brand new 225 Buick. I worked during days and Billy worked at night while I kept his car. Billy met this new girl who seemed pretty nice and looked pretty good too. Well after only a few weeks one Sunday morning Billy came home limping with his foot bandaged by a doctor, professionally done you no. I asked him what happened to your foot. He said with a shy grin on his face, Jane threw an iron at me and it hit me right on my foot, is it broken, no there is a small fracture though. I said dang boy, wa kind of gal is dat? The next week, same thing except this time he had a t-shirt tied around his head, I said gait day boy you better quit going over there. He said come on Arvanie lets ride back over there with me I want you to tell me what you think. We rode back over to Jane's house and she was in a friendly mood so I asked her, Jane what seems to be the problem with you and Billy? She spoke right up, Arvanie I told Billy that I don't need no man, I said what? I don't need no man I got me a woman. I said woe, Billy lets go, we got in the car and Billy was just sitting there thinking, looking out of the window. I said Billy what are you doing let's go, wa do you think I autta do Arvanie I love her now. You is in a heap a trouble now boy because she do not want you, she wants the same thing that you want, a woman, she's gay, oh- you don't reckin I can change her, as pretty as she is, no son that's some pain that you will have to deal with for the rest of your life because love doesn't go away, it eases into a different realm but it will always be with you.

Love is the most powerful emotion on earth and in heaven; love only comes to you for someone when God determines that he will send it. It comes unexpectedly from out of the universe where God stores it. No one decides whom they will fall in love with and love is almost always unequal, no two partners love each other equally. I've never known any two people who fall in love for their first time and the partnership last, that kind of love will have the capacity to grow to be too great, and it will ultimately come between you and God. If one can fall in love with someone and be able to trust equally as well, there is absolutely nothing that those two cannot do without God, and that is something that will never happen. God is the creator and decides who falls in love that will last! Love last beyond the grave indefinitely and there absolutely nothing that you can do about. When God gives you his spirit at conception it never changes, it grows right along with you. When I was in the third grade I was in love with the young girl who was in the Christmas play with me, we three Kings however most people try to tell me that I don't know what love is at seven years old, well she remained my girl until I went to Terrell's bay junior high and high school. The girls at Terrell's Bay were not shy at all they took me from Lynn and six months later another girl came and ask me if she could be my girl and a few months later they kept coming, I never said no because none of those young girls were giving me anything any way. Now when I got in the tenth grade in the spring of 1964 I was sixteen years old and love took on a different meaning. I was dancing every day to the sweet sounding music of Jr. Walker's, "hot chow "and I could care less if my girl Lisa was in love for the first time or not, in fact I knew that it wasn't, but when the dance competition was over and I wasn't able to hold her in my arms I felt terribly lonesome and sad at the same time, I was uncomfortable until we started dating and then happiness and peace returned. But let me tell you, when I found out that she was my cousin and I was not supposed to have her love, I had to walk away in tremendous pain, unlike any feeling that I have ever had until this day. God was watching over us and preparing me for my future, I've had no sad thoughts or anger towards anyone for that relationship in fact I'm proud and happy to have those memories, they bring me joy and allow me to recapture the heart and mind of a sixteen year old ED Graves.

Samson's purpose in life was to eradicate the Philistines, each time we find evidence in our Bibles of the children of Isreal being disobedient or following other Gods, he sent the Philistines to reek havoc on the lives and crops of the Israelites. When Samson came in contact with Delilah at age thirty six he had a feeling of entitlement because he came to the realization through prayer after losing both his first love along with his only and best friend, that God never intended for him to have a child or family, he was a Nazarene with a distinct purpose only and that purpose restricted him from a family life because he had to never have to worry about his family or to leave a child behind to be murdered. He was restricted from drinking wine or alcohol, he was never supposed to touch a dead body of any kind, and he was never supposed to cut his hair or shave, his head was to be Holy unto the Lord all of his life, but no one told him as a child these things. After Samson killed the multitude of Philistines in the auditorium with the two pillars that he dreamed and saw visions of all of his life, they seem to have dropped off of the face of the earth, God used the philistines to terrorize the Israelites and when he got ready he sent Samson to demolish them entirely. Although they have never been a threat anymore they have merged into other cultures because all of the men were wiped out. I believe that that is what happens to all cultures when God's purpose for their lives cease to be a major player in society anymore. It is the natural order of things to evolve and die out, that's what's going to have to happen to people who are bigots both black and white.

I'm in my six stage of life a senior at age 63; when I become 76 years old I will begin my seventh and final stage, however I could die anytime it is up to God's plan for my life. I take care of my health and exercise both my mind and body and leave the rest in God's hands. I still have definitive desires and plans- goals to accomplish and work to be done, I am a happy man I do have some regrets and some things that I would have changed if I could have but I would rather be where I am than to go back a to try and relive some things a different way. I've lived to see my people evolve from the lowest human condition on earth, slavery- and its memory is still fresh in my mind, the stories told to me by my Grandfather, my Dad and uncles. I have been asked the question by a white associate that I used to work with" the South will rise again isn't it ED," I said who do you plan to have for slaves this time, the idea of you getting black slaves is ridiculous at best, no people in the History of the world has ever come from being slaves to rise to the Whitehouse, the President of the United States of America without even having to shed blood in all out

War but never the less black people have shed blood in a non-violent premise that God has endorsed, it is his time now to do what he will and the future looks great. The youth in the world are going to schools together without any problems with race at all, the concern for them is survival and finding competent jobs to support their families. Sooner rather than later there will be an explosion of new inventions and discoveries are on the rise, the computer has seriously changed the world forever. Now there will always be the need for a segment of the population who will have to do the menial low level jobs like garbage and lawn service has become lucrative for anyone to become self employed and do really well financially. Although it is quite visible who are going to have to take the low level low paying jobs, the school dropout rate is as high as it ever was and the prison population is growing by leaps and bounds. The secret obstacles being placed on the lives of young blacks is disturbing, traps are being sat and targeted to place Felonies on the records of any black person at will. No one deliberately parks and leave a brand new Cadillac in the poorest neighborhoods in cities of the US. where poor blacks and Hispanics live other than to rack up as many Felonies on them as they can every week. If they didn't park the car there and leave the keys in it with the door open hundreds of young people could go on with their lives uninvaded and go on to live productive lives only if they had gotten past that one day in their lives. I've seen the show Cop's every day and witness the Police planting a Police woman in the neighborhood and ask the men if they wish to purchase sex, if the Police will deliberately plant a Policeman or woman in order to trap an individual what makes you think that they want plant guns, drugs and other contraband undercover.

As hard as it is to find a good job these days to support a family with no record at all leaves no chance once they get young black men in the prison system. The only people who are hurting from the mortgage foreclosures crises are poor people, now that the rich has taken their homes those people have to go back further behind the successful all American dream than they were before they invested in the first place. It's a process which will effect generations poor people in years to come. Such tactics have been planned forty and fifty years in advance. What do you do when you've lost everything that you've worked for all of your life. Once you have aged all prospects of hope and a good livelihood is gone, there is no lateral movements to explore and take advantage of the dream is gone for you, your children and Grandchildren in just one trick; It is a feeling of having your pocket picked but for bigger losses and no way to regain or recapture what you've lost. There is no conscience in the minds of the unending greed of others, money is addictive and there is no end in sight as to how much is enough. I went to see the movie "Django" staring Jamie Fox the day after Christmas in 2012 and enjoyed it immensely, Django went back into the deep South to rescue his wife who had been taken and sold away from him while they put him in prison to be whipped, sold and re-sold at will. The theater was about sixty percent black and forty percent white viewers in Columbia with no interruptions when Jamie begun to kill the white slave holders brutally. Well, in Florence a little further down the road Southeast In the Pee Dee, my brother told me that when the killing started by Jamie all of the whites got up and left the theater. All along while we watched the white slave owners whipping the young defenseless black women and sexually exploiting them everything was fine.

121

Some of this same kind of activity was told to me by my uncles and Grandfather, if a white slave owner was handy with this kind of treachery and brutality against the black slaves, during harvest time when the tobacco was being cured in the tobacco barns at night, somehow the slave owner just happen to come up missing, he got burned up in the barn. Some were found floating in their fish ponds while fishing, the big paybacks were spaced out so that great suspicion was avoided. There were hunting accidents which were not responded to as suspicious. It does not matter who you are and how long it seems to take, you will reap just what you sow, and reaping under those conditions are horrible and hard to swallow.

The Bible says that you must treat people as you would like to be treated and to love thy neighbor as we love ourselves. When you truly love someone it is a good thing, but make no mistake, to love someone is fundamentally intrinsically different than being in love with someone. Al Green wrote a song called love and happiness, love will make you stay up "all night long", love will make you do right and make you do wrong. If there is someone that you think about at least once per week every week, even though there is absolutely nothing that you want from that person sexually or otherwise, no physical contact even, if you think about that person at least once per week, you will always be in love with that individual! Now let me offer you some valuable advice, you must consider how it is that you think about this person and ask yourself, why did God send this kind of love to you for this person?

All power comes from God, even the evil doers and those who practice witchcraft, it is God's power being used incorrectly by the wrong people and for the wrong reasons. The Bible said that there were people who know the principals of power and can use that knowledge to do evil things but don't worry, it will all come back to them. If God decided that he wanted you to experience the power of love with a certain person, it is for a very special reason, there is something that you have not considered. There is some spiritual connection from the invisible world from long ago that God wants you to see. The spirit that we have within us has always been, and will always be, it will never die, only the body that the real you is housed in will die and just "perhaps", once your memory has been erased your spirit, the real you will be given a new assignment if you overcome all of your obstacles in this life.

We are supposed to love God with all your heart, all your soul, all your mind and all of your strength, the only way that I've found to be able to do that to its fullest is to give God complete control of my mind, my heart, my soul and all of my strength, I asked God to take complete control of my mind heart soul and strength and teach me how it is to be done. Once I have surrendered completely, I concentrate on my faith, I have to be as sure that the thing that I have asked for is given to me to the degree that there can be absolutely no doubt. Today is Thursday evening at five twenty pm and I know that tomorrow is Friday, and that tomorrow I'm going to" Golden Coral" for dinner (smile). It has some of everything that I like and there is no waiting! If you truly love someone it is impossible to be angry with that person for more than one hour, the rest is just acting. I know just who each of my brothers have ever been in love with, just for experimentation I call that person's name in conversation just out of the blue and watch their eyes not only light up but widen also. There are different realms of love and it exists at deferent degrees, you will come to love some people more than others and there's no apparent reason for it, no explanation what so ever. On the cross Jesus loved both Titus and dumb ass, "Dumachass" the two young boys that he met at the outer gates leaving Egypt whom he told that they would wind up on a tree however Titus had since enough to know that no normal baby could possibly know all of the family members of theirs going back one thousand years and better. That baby Jesus was God and there is no doubt. Why would the almighty God send himself down, his only son to be born in a smelly horse and mule stable when he created the whole world and everything in it, all of the money that's in the world, and whatever form, Gold coin hammered by the man that he sent into the world, the silver, copper diamonds, oils, uranium everything, what does God have to prove to anyone? He owns all of the cattle, you name it, it all belongs to God and there has never been a single penny to ever leave the earth, it is still here in some form or the other. Two years before Jesus was to ever be born God sent three rich Kings with Gold and other valuables to support his dark complexioned parents, Joseph and Mary for many years. He instructed his own star to shine brighter than any other for two years, so why do you think that he would've said well I think I'll send my beloved son the be born lower than his own children, they all were born in houses. Jesus was never poor he simply chose not to carry the man made money of his children in his pockets when he could command fish to bring money to him. The reason that Jesus cursed the fig tree which is still cursed today; the fig tree is the only fruit tree that does not blossom before it bears fruit today, no blossoms ever, just figs; Each morning when Jesus awakened there would be fruit to sprout up overnight and a cushioned grass would grow into a soft mattress for him, when Satan tampered with the fig tree so that it wouldn't have breakfast for Jesus the next morning, Jesus cursed the fig tree all the way back to its creational foundations and that curse remains partially today as a sign; One day Jesus was said to have been riding on a mule through the forest and the foul-partridge flew up quickly and its fluttering wings scarred the mule, the mule bucked and threw King Jesus to the ground, Jesus got up and cursed the mule such that he would be the only animal created to never be able to reproduce after its kind. He cursed the partridge such that they would never again be able to fly above the tree tops; And so it is!

In our Bible, the book of Luke Chapter 8 verse two and three, there is significant information in many books explaining the preparation that God made for Jesus before he ever came into the Earth. For instance Joanna, the wife of "Chuza" is a phrase of factual information that always perk and peek my interest tremendously. King Herod as all Kings had in his employ a chief Stewart- some Kings used the title Prime Minister whose main duties are to keep an accurate account of all of the Kings riches and possessions of value in a record book that only he has privilege to and knowledge of its whereabouts. The chief Stewart hires or recommends the scribe to be the Kings personal writer and record keeper of events throughout the Kings reign. Chuza had a large and beautiful mansion with maids, handmaidens, concubines and the like for his pleasure. Joanna, his wife along with her friend Susanna prepared the room in the east end of Chuza's house for Jesus and his disciples and other guest on the third floor, a portion of the house that Chuza never had any reason to go near for any reason, 20,000 square feet was more than he ever needed for just he and his wife. Just imagine, King Herod had hired bounty hunters looking all over the lands surrounding Jerusalem and beyond. Jesus had his last supper in the very house of the King Herod who was seriously trying to kill him, the same as his father who tried to Kill him at birth, the home of his top man! Throughout the life and ministry of Jesus there was always someone who prepared the way for Jesus until it came to his first cousin John the Baptist. All of Jesus disciples who left their homes to follow him received one hundred fold all of the necessities of life and then some. Peter's wife told him once when he came home for a visit that she could not run out of anything, every time she went into her cupboards for flour, meal or oils the container was always overflowing. The star that shinned so brightly the night that Jesus was born had to have been outside of town in the cave otherwise if he was born in the stable in town as the fairy tale of his birth suggest, the entire town and everyone else would have seen it and went directly to Jesus. God made great and thorough preparations thousands of years before he sent his only son in the Earth to die at the appointed time. The entire three hours that Jesus hung on the cross all of the animals on Earth stood with these heads hung down in reverence to the King of Kings! Jesus cursed the fig tree but he lifted it for bearing fruit because he said in the beginning that man could eat of every tree except of the tree of good and evil. The mule's curse still stands but God gave him an unusual gift, the mule and donkey are the only creations that are able to see all four feet at once, the mule never stumbles as the horse does. There are Bible books that did not get canonized with great information, there is a book written on all of the disciples and eight of the twelve sons of Jacob, the book of Thomas is fascinating. King Solomon wrote three thousand manuscripts, one thousand songs and the seventh and twenty seventh book of the Psalms. I've seen books in the library of an old Attorney who was a client of mine that Solomon described the procedure on how to build a city, how and when to plant certain crops and it was Solomon who separated the fouls from all other animals and categorized them. Solomon gave the Holy of Holies to his son Menaleke by the queen of Sheba in Ethiopia and it is housed in a guarded Temple today by Ethiopian monks, however these are black people so the Historians dismiss that fact.

Today we are transitioning from a past that was horrible and disgusting but only a people with the determination to survive and thrive as the African American could have endured the obstacles that we have overcome. Powerful wills to live if only so that their descendants would live a free and productive life. We are the only race of people who have relatives in every Country on Earth, just dropped off and sold at will on every Island that you can think of. God told Abraham that everywhere that his feet tread(walked) that he would give that land to him and his descendants. President Obama is the son of an African King, and Mandela is the son of a King in South Africa. Yes we see confederate flags flying in a lost cause but it is still the history of the whites. The word "slave and nigger" is the history of the blacks and it will never go away and I am one who does not want the word nigger to go away, the word nigger carries us all the way back to Africa and the Niger river where I believe that the spelling changed by the Southern white Slave traders. We must change the way that we think about the word that hurt so many people, why does it hurt you? Does the word nigger Booker T. Washington, Fredrick Douglas, Nigger Muhammad Ali, Joe Frazier and nigger Barack Obama, why would they hurt you if you only learned to embrace everything that comes with slavery you would see that it is only a part of our history that is painful to think of. The word nigger brings laughter through joy and pain.

Today the world looks different through my eyes, the eyes of a senior citizen 63 years old who finds it difficult to find new and exciting things to do, very few friends that I fit into their realms of life's expectations to come. I remember when I was younger when I first began to acknowledge the people in Churches and communities who belonged to the old age category of life, ages 76 and older. These are folks who seemingly only have Church services and functions to look forward to each week. However they do seem to be happy and getting along in life just fine, and then there are those who continue to work in their chosen professions and are doing great, they have both happiness and joy on their faces. I'm happy to have found the perfect Church for me and I've developed some wonderful relationships as well, and now certainly there is my former high school teacher and her cool husband "Jack" that I enjoy seeing every Sunday. Let's use the alternate name Mrs. Velvet; she still has the most beautiful velvet voice that I remember from high school. Every boy in my class had a crush on her and other boys in various classes as well, she was a red bone you know with beautiful legs and wide hips but not too wide. When cool Jack came and captured her heart we were all saddened because it was the last we ever saw her. My Pastor is a charismatic and handsome man who brings excitement to the pulpit and church as well, he can easily make you laugh and continue bringing his messages in order and fruitful scriptures, I must tell you that he is one who can really sing also. My Deacon is a cool H. R. whom I am very proud of his life's work. It feels good to belong to a Church family with so many wonderful people who enjoy church services, and I'll never forget my sister the Rev. D. J. Rev. J. R. I'm ministering through books now and in the near future I hope to be doing moves and theater entertainment, a new and exciting field for me at this stage of my life. The future does not look very good for our children as far as the employment situation which still seems to only improve sparingly, this is the first generation to expect to do worst financially than their parents. As I mentioned in the previous chapter we are in a transitional stage of development in the US. And pain always show up in the obstacles of moving forward when the circumstances of living are different, a new way of thinking is at hand and new business development is eminent. On TTRACC Bible Business College will do its part in this movement and I'm very excited about the future in this Country. There is no such thing as a safe job anymore and there is always joy and pain in progress. Young adults coming out of Colleges years after with very little hope and expectation of finding their perfect job with the income to match it.

When African Americans came out of Slavery their expectations were so much greater in those days than it is today coming out of College. Moving with freedoms that they never had to go anywhere that they wanted to both in and out of this Country. Any job that they took was a tremendous increase from what they all were used to, nothing at all, never being able to buy new clothes for themselves their spouses or their children. Being able to buy the kinds of food that you wanted to eat all of your life was finally at hand which brought about unspeakable joy around the world. Different races of people coming into the United States today have a different perspective all together in what lies ahead for them and their families. The world is watching the White House, who can be next to be the most power and most criticized as Obama has been. God is allowing him to get all things done right and done well even though he is being fought, criticized and downright blocked for some of his programs. White America does not want it known that a son of a people who were former slaves to be able to do his job with such ease and destined processes. The time has come for another people to get their chance to advance this Country into the future which brings with it great changes in the thinking of America. This is the promise land and absolutely no one who has ever came to America ever wants to leave. It is certainly going to be a bitter pill for white Americans to swallow, they have been taught their history of fighting Wars and taking this land for themselves and now the very people whom they brought here to build and cultivate roads, canals, buildings to include the White House and now there is one of the people who were on the very bottom only one hundred and fifty years ago are on the very top today, January 2013 miraculous and incredible. When I think about what my ancestors went through so that I could be born free, today my mind is constantly moving, trying to find the next step on the track that God created for me to follow and piece together the good that I can do for the Glory of God. White Americans came to America, most were criminals and misfits, came with the express idea to take this beautiful land from the Indians and enslave them to build and cultivate into the most powerful and richest Country on Earth, however the Indians would rather fight and die than to be enslaved in their own lands. So today the Indians are the most humbled and locked away people in this Country. Then the white Americans fought the Revolutionary War against their homeland, Great Brittan with the help of the Indians and the Black slaves whom they brought from Africa to do all of the work while white Americans sat and watched their bank accounts grow into millions of dollars which most still exist today but only for the fittest few. That is how this Country became the greatest and richest power on Earth. Rome, comparatively speaking was the innovative powerful Country that every major Country has immulated (copied) as far as roads and building structures, mail system and welfare system as long as two thousand years ago Rome ruled the known world for six hundred years. And do you know why Rome fell? Why ED? Each time Jesus performed a miracle raising the dead, healing the blind and the lame, causing the Roman soldiers to become converted because they spied on everything that he did and ultimately a Roman Governor had Jesus Killed. When Julius Caesar found out that Pontius Pilate killed the only man that could heal both he and his wife of terminal illnesses he summoned Pilate to Rome to behead him which is the most dishonorable death for a soldier, Pilate fell on his own sword stabbing himself in the stomach. Rome fell because they killed the only son of God; Every City in every State has named their cities after the Roman Empire, there is a Greenville in every State in America I believe. In 1861(6+1=7) There are seven letters in the name "Lincoln", Slavery was worth more money than all of the banks, stock companies, all of the cotton and rice, tobacco plantations put together in 1861, the Confederate whites would fight again today if they thought that they could get their slaves back. Now let me tell you why slavery fell for the whites in America, why ED? They brought Martin. L.

King Jr., Joe Louis, Rosa Parks, Muhammad Ali, Opra Winfrey and all of the great and powerful blacks on ships to America, there is seven letters in Arvanie, smile;

In 1861 William Wrigley Jr. was born in Philadelphia Pennsylvania, made a fortune selling one penny per stick gum, he purchased Wrigley field and the Chicago Cubs, in 1932 during the depression he amassed 34 Million dollars (34,000,000) when he died. He bought Catalina Island in California which is one of the riches Islands in America today, a beautiful resort where you can only rent golf carts to get around town in, a permit to purchase a car will take waiting ten to twelve years to get a permit to buy. Let us all understand that it took the cooperation of many and powerful whites to help get the slaves free but let us also understand that the Civil War would have certainly been lost to the Confederacy if it had not been for the fighting black slaves and free blacks, so why would you think that the word nigger would bother me if the word slave doesn't. I remember when I was a child running and playing in plowed open fields and often bruising and small cuts to my feet and legs causing sores, well where ever the sore was, something would always hit me directly in the sore of all the other places on my body, the object found its way to hit me where it would certainly hurt me the most, that is exactly what white Americans do, they hit you with the one word that hurts blacks. No one cares if a Chinese or Japanese, or Native American called you a nigger, it is because they are not more powerful than you. Those races of people are shorter than and not as strong as you are, Kung fu or not and they never had the power to enslave or sell you. White Americans are the richest and most powerful people on Earth today, they have the wealth but that is about to change, the computer age is upon us and a new millennium; Can you imagined what America would be like without rice, well rice came from Africa and the only people who were able to withstand the heat and malaria, other illnesses which came as a result of working all day in one hundred degree weather with knee high water and the no how to grow rice were black Africans; Brook Green Gardens is one of the most beautiful former rice plantations in South Carolina near Myrtle Beach. Ever year people come from all over the world to see Brook Green Gardens and its many splendors, it is an outdoor museum with sights that cannot be explained, you must see it for yourself on hwy 17 South from Myrtle Beach towards Charleston. All kinds of battles were fought over the Charleston Harbor and slave drop off to be sold. The whites are still angry at the blacks because they thought that ignorant black slaves would always want to work, serve and slave for them, love them that much! That hate never goes away it will be present until the entire haters die out. Watermelons are an African citrus brought here by Africans so of course we love watermelon, and now let us discuss "music".

Gospel, the Blues and rhythm and blues came from Africa. Music is a form of prayer it touches you and others deep inside. White slave traders brought people like Aretha Franklin, Sam Cooke, and Isaac Hayes, Edna Gamble Cooke, Smoky Robinson, the Ojays and many other musical artists. Elvis Presley changed the world by being white and sounding black, he said himself that he learned all of his music from black people. Tina Marie did the same thing when she coupled with Rick James, all great musicians has changed the world just like sports. Paul Simon went to South

Africa in 1987 and performed with African groups during the struggle with apartheid and brought about a wondrous change in the thinking of the world. But we still have millions of people like Michelle Bachman the female candidate for President on a Republican platform who still thinks that black people were better off when we were in slavery, don't make me laugh, just how stupid can a grown woman get without falling completely off the face of the Earth. People like Richard Pryor, Sidney Poitier and Bill Cosby took what they had on the inside and made millions, no one taught them to perform. God has placed wondrous gifts and talents in all of us to find and cultivate so that we can change the world piece by piece. John DuPont got wealthy and changed the world, where did he get the start up money to make "gun powder". The only thing that will make some people happy is to bring back Elvis and Slavery! Too many people are waiting for something out of the atmosphere to come and bless them, and make them rich. When Solomon Jackson, the black preacher who won the $256,000,000 lottery, all sorts of tickets are being sold today to people who cannot afford to spend money that way but I guest everyone needs something exciting to look forward too. I'm not one to stand in the way of anyone finding happiness no matter it seems to me. Just to think about where we have come from as a people, the very same words that Martin L. King spoke in his I have a dream speech has come to pass.

Fifty years from now the most prevalent language spoken in American will be Spanish, I believe that black people will be making their own cars within the next twenty five years, phenomenal changes will take place in this promise land that is not ours, it belongs to God and no one knows what is on his time table. The meek will inherit the Earth and black people are far from being meek, you have to be like unto a child to be meek and who will that be? Tremendous business ownership and self-employment has to take place, the jobs that were lost to the over Seas markets will never come back. The jobs which are available to our young people today will not pay the rent and buy a car. It is sad but we are in transition and sad things happen during a transitional period but when we come out on the other side things will be great. The wealth will have certainly moved from its present status and as I said previously, no money has ever left the Earth, just changed hands. When I was seventeen years old I had to leave home and go North to find a job and now everyone who can come back South are coming back with problems and obstacles to overcome.

In 1966 when I graduated from high school gas was thirty cents per gallon, cigarettes were thirty cents per pack and I quit smoking when they went to one dollar per pack thirty five years ago. The only jobs in Rains and Marion County has always been cropping tobacco and picking cotton, seems like a very long time ago, seems like one hundred and fifty years ago. We drive and walk past people every day who want to put us or anyone who is weak enough back into slavery, and they never thought that God had his reasons for allowing it to happen, you can't just go to great big Africa and buy, steal or borrow that many people for over four hundred years, the most powerful and greatest fighting people on the Earth. During my studies and research many years ago concerning the Civil war, there was a steam ship leaving Virginia with fourteen hundred beaten men after Robert E. Lee surrendered at Appomattox court house in April 1865. These men were going home to South Carolina and other Southern States to round up blacks who were dumb enough they thought and resume their lives of riches and pleasure, well as the ship got about fifty miles out into the ocean the boiler burst, exploded and killed each and everyone on board. President Lincoln said that anyone who couldn't see the hand of God in the battle of Gettysburg had to be completely blind. All the confederate States had to do from the beginning was to agree to Lincoln's proposal of just staying in the Union, they could have kept their slaves, President Lincoln had no intention of freeing any slaves if he didn't have to, his main purpose was initially to keep the Union intact, however God wanted to kill off some bigots and set his people free after his set timing! South Carolina was the place where everything was to begin, the slave harbor and trading post in Charleston was the new "EGYPT". God sent Abraham Lincoln as his next Moses and just like Pharaoh and all of his army were killed, so was Lincoln and the armies of both the North and South. America has always been the promise land and no one people will ever be able to hold power forever under no circumstances. This land will be cleansed and washed until it becomes like God wants it to be. People are dying in Cities all over this Country every day and no one can explain it. There are forces from the invisible world of evil spirits involved and only God can fix the problem. There is no apparent answer to the question of gang violence, there is absolutely too much money in the drug and gun trade. The gang bangers have found a way to live as best they can with the riches they earn through the death of their comrades, as soon as one is killed there are five others ready and waiting to take their place and the opportunity to become rich and powerful. It is sad and

I'm glad that I was not born in times such as these to have to grow up and go to school with every other student that you past by has a gun in their back pack.

At this juncture I would like to share with you my views and ideas of the slave mind once they received the opportunity to meet face to face their oppressors on the battle field on equal footing with guns and bayonet's in their hands. If I found myself on a battlefield as the slaves did with the taste of freedom in their minds, after being beaten and seen others and my family members both men and women tied to a tree in public and whipped until their backs were cut through to the bone and laying open and bleeding, to have seen my brothers and parents sold off without any though by the slave owner, it would be just like it was when Samson saw the jawbone of the ass and he slew one thousand soldiers with it with ease. Having the opportunity to wear a brand new pair of Army boots and new uniform with matching blue colors for the first time in my life, trust me, that in itself would have been enough for me to make the decision without any hesitation that I would rather die five times fighting my enemy rather than to go back to being a slave. Just knowing that back on the plantation my entire family is being held by people who own them and my children who hate them just because they are black and want to be free, emptying their pockets with the wealth from the power that he holds over them. Anytime that I see the confederate flag wherever it is it reminds me that my ancestors cried and prayed every day and every night that one day their children or grandchildren would experience the taste of freedom and this flag is a symbol of that deliverance. That flag brought out the hate and anger that had been penned up for over four hundred years and no one was going to cheat them out of the opportunity to do what their ancestors who had died long ago hoping for that day to come. Absolutely no one will fight as hard with the determination to win freedom for their people as a slave who has in his mind that there is a white man with the power to take away the new clothing and the feeling of freedom that it brings than a fighting black man with the inherent where withal to fight hand to hand combat, but has a gun with the ability to kill from a long ways off. The slaves knew they were valuable but had no idea that they valued more than all of the trains, all of the cars and livestock, all of the stock markets and banks and insurance companies and real-estate put together! The white slave owners and the whites who could not even afford just one slave were just as willing to die to keep their way of life. To be white in the United States of America where the white ancestors died fighting the British in the War, the Indians to steal the land, had Statues erected all over this Country and Cities and streets named after their ancestors years ago, they could do anything that they wanted to with the black female and work and whip any black human being at his own pleasure. Didn't have to get a glass of drinking water, just order any slave anywhere and anytime, "hey you nigger" go and get me a glass of water and be quick about it!

At night while sleeping in their own beds in camp for the first time in their lives the free slave had time to think for himself and his future for the first time in their lives no matter how long or short it lasted. Anything that had ever hurt him physically or mentally showed up with great antipathy in the mind. Each and every slave new without any doubt that they would kill as many Confederates as possible without any hesitation before they died, that was their greatest wish. The Confederate soldiers came on the battle field with the attitude that the black slave would throw down their weapons at the sight of the white soldier not knowing that it has always been in the slave's mind even on plantations that if he ever got the chance and not be caught, there was no way that the white man could beat him in a fair fight. The slave was always lifting something heavy and always working which kept his body fit while the white man was always lounging around drinking, not having to lift a finger to pick up a chicken breast. The white soldiers were no match when they got on the battle field, the slave had been waiting for that opportunity all of their lives with the hope that one day they would get their chance and right here right now this battle is mine. If you find yourself in a battle with a black man who doesn't mind dying, you have got yourself a tough row to hoe!

We always knew that when Muhammad Ali fought a white fighter he was not interested in a quick knockout, Ali had it in his mind to humiliate the opponent with capricious flurries from angles to cut and cause deep bruising underneath the skin. He used all kinds of abusive language to raise the anger in the white fighters so that they would rush in and get pummeled furiously causing the most pain.

In 1866 George Westinghouse used the wealth that his father raised from slaves to have the opportunity to invest in the development of the trains and in 1837 Andrew Carnegie got involved also and made millions, however it was John D. DuPont in 1802 who really changed the world when he developed Gun Powder! Gun Powder allowed the whites to come to America and take anything that they wanted, the Indians land, beautiful lakes and streams. Great mountains and solemn valleys, picturesque sights of snowy hills and mountains, green foliage just waiting to be touched. Guns with gun powder allows anyone to kill at will. But there is a great need and pleasure to be had with guns, I have a few myself. Every Island that you visit on vacations you will certainly see what slavery has done and left the black inhabitants with. I do not enjoy seeing the poverty everywhere you go in travel to the beautiful Caribbean's and Virgin Islands, there is always the poor blacks begging for change and such, slavery has left them hopeless and depending on tourist as their only income. In every City in America there is a desolate poor community of beggars; it is the only means of survival in many cases. But to those of us who have decided to succeed anyway, there is nothing more powerful than an idea that has come into God's timing. When you begin to walk on the track that God has created just for you, you will encounter no rivals.

When Jesus started his ministry after his baptism by John the Baptist, his first cousin, it is the only place in our Bibles that you can bear witness to the Holy spirit, which sat upon his shoulder like a dove and the heavens opened up when God spoke and said, this is my beloved son-in whom I 'm well pleased! It is the only time that all three God heads showed up at one place at the same time. This same three came down to the Earth when God decided to make man-Adam, he brought his kingdom down to the Garden of Eden and said, let us make man in our own image. What is truly fascinating is the day that Jesus fed the five thousand. Research and study revealed to me the fact that the day before he fed the five thousand Jesus visited the home of the little boy who brought the lunch box containing the two fish and five barley loaves of bread. The boy's father had been sick for three years and could not walk so his son fished and supported the two of them. Jesus healed the boy's father and both the son and his father were well pleased. The next day the little boy went fishing and caught enough to feed he and his father with some extra for his new friend Jesus. The boy was the only one among the five thousand men to include the twelve disciples to think enough about Jesus to bring him some cooked fish after his sermon. Jesus also knew that the boy would bring him something to eat so when he asked who has food to eat, the little boy did not hesitate to share his lunch with Jesus. The Disciples did not believe that it was possible to feed three people much less the five thousand, however the act that Jesus was instructing was simply that you "must start" take the first step. When they took the cooked fish that the boy had prepared and broke it, Jesus had already seen in his prayer a seafood buffet with endlessness and boundlessness in his mind, just like it is in Heaven, everything is endless and boundless in the Kingdom's invisible world.

Sadly though, it is unusual to me when men and women live on the same earth and see the evolving and transitional occurrences on Earth so differently. In the 1700's in Barbados and other Islands there was a teaching practice among the white race a methodology which was designed specifically to break the spirit of a black slave, to confine his thinking only to work in sugar cane fields from sun up to sun down six days a week. These men were trained in this profession as a livelihood which was supposed to exist in the world at large forever, absolutely no thought or concern for the black slave at all. Christian white men and women marveled in the luxurious life of bliss while the slave worked himself and herself to death, barely reaching the age of forty five. The first five or six Governors in South Carolina and North Carolina came from

Barbados! In 1966 when I graduated from high school I couldn't even begin to think of such a thing as a black President. I had to leave the South in order to find a job that did not have anything to do with farm work on the white man's farm, our farm was lost. Some black people were discriminating against other blacks as bad or worse than the whites did.

Today jobs with good pay are finding their way into the South, bringing many people with them and who knows what tomorrow will bring, it is difficult to predict two years in advance what turn your livelihood will take. When I was visiting Baltimore in the mid-nineties there was a severe sadness on the streets of the Cities in the North. A complete opposite has taken place as far as jobs go. The streets are lined and crowded with unemployed black people who are either hooked on drugs or alcohol, all of the hustling and bustling of the working class of a few years ago have fallen, all of the large companies have just left the City leaving behind empty dilapidated buildings. People's furniture has been sat out on the streets leaving an ugly sight to see, they have been put out of their apartment with no place to go but back South where their parents came from sixty years ago and longer. The rich and powerful are setting the course and future for those people with no regard for their way of life for the next sixty years when they will reverse the trend.

Treyvon Martin

Growing up in Rains sc. in the late fifties and early sixties I witnessed the dangers of being black in America. I cropped tobacco in fields alongside white boys in friendly atmospheric conditions when the Sun was bearing down to almost and sometimes one hundred degrees. Over the weekend we went to our own black churches, home to a scrumptious Sunday dinner and later in the evening —out on our Sun- day night dates, only to wake up on Monday mornings and find myself in a tobacco field with those same white boys who were friends and schoolmates of boys who invited a young black kid-my age to Myrtle Beach, get him drunk and then cut his face and body up terribly with a knife or "straight razor".

Many weekends we heard on the news that men from neighborhoods very close to my home, the white policemen would randomly pick up a black man as he was simply walking home alongside the road and take him to jail and lock him up with his hands cuffed behind his back and hang him with the bed sheets, show his hands cuffed behind his back and report that "he hangs himself". In a couple of hours in the tobacco field though, we would all be talking, laughing and telling jokes but the feelings of anger stayed with me for a long time after woods, some until this day. It seems to have always been such a state of mind that those things would always be with us until the time and day would come when retaliation would be inevitable. We all remember in the black communities when the young four- teen year old black kid was taken and beaten unmercifully and then shot numerous times and his body was thrown in a pond simply for looking a white woman in the eye.

When Treyvon Martin was shot and killed just last year, all of my memories reflected back to all of the black people innocently killed simply for being black throughout my lifetime. Amazingly we move on without carrying that baggage of anger and hostility which certainly will wear you down. I have found that it takes too much of your time and energy to stay in an angered state of mind against someone. Anger slows and wears you down over time so I get rid of my anger as soon as I can. I chose to be happy on my own initiatives, I simply change the way that I think about things that bother me and move the negative thought to another place. The thought of Treyvon Martin reminds me that some white people are still angry that when they see black people it angers them that we are their old money that got away from them and they still want their slaves back!

I will demonstrate my analogy of life right here-right now by switching to a mode of thought that brings me joy and happiness. You see all that I have to do is to recall my memories of Rains-and Crawford town, or my early years when I used to box every day at my elementary school with my cousin Seldon. The days when I saw the beautiful Lisa my first love and the young girl with the Indian sounding name. Sometimes I wish that I could put some people back into their young bodies-my first girlfriend that people keep trying to tell me that I didn't know what love was when I was in the third grade, well, what is it that blossoms in my heart each time I think of them.

There was a fellow who married my cousin who still lives in Rains today who always made me laugh uncontrollably when he often talked about his love for wife and he told me many things "not" to do when I got married someday. We called this fellow "Lil-Buddy", and the thing that was so seriously fascinating about Lil Buddy was that he was the greatest baseball pitcher- in the same league as Satchel Page during the Jackie Robinson era. Lil Buddy could throw a baseball and make it brake around the corner of a house, on either side of a shotgun house early in the morning. He was so good that hours later he could get half "drunk" and do the absolute same thing, the same curve with the same velocity and power! He pitched to me in the clay hole, threw three pitches, all with different bouncing breaking pitches, I never got to swing an either one, any day. No team ever came to Rains and won anything because "Lil Buddy was there! People used to say-there is no need to take your team to Rains unless you don't want to get your ass kicked!

CHAPTER EIGHT

Racism

Unfortunately and invariably racism existed since the beginning when the black African lost their inherent power over all species all over the world. The Black African is the most hated by whites under the Sun, whites being the most powerful and the richest in the world. Whites have taken the culture that they wanted out of Africa and discarded the rest, claiming that we have no History other than oral when the Egyptians and Africans in the Sudan and Timbuctu wrote in books and on every constructed building in those Countries and still exist today. In current times (today) We know that the police force was not needed in America until the year 1641, 21 years after the indentured slaves in Jamestown Virginia were freed and left to go back to Charleston South Carolina after staying on a few extra years to earn money to buy wagons, plows, tools etc. to buy land to feed and support their families. Black slaves could never run away and mingle into white society because of their easily identified black skin color. Our black skin color is the very thing today when seen by a white police officer gives radiant rise and excitement to white police officers to harass, arrest and kill black people both woman and men. Just a week ago Sunday a white police officer shot a young black man "seven times" in the back at point blank range with his three children inside the car he had been driving. There were several witness standing nearby watching as the four police officers who tassied and punched him!

Only a few months ago "George Floyd" was killed when a white police officer kneeled on his neck until he was dead with many people watching helplessly. The difference now than the KKK hanging and killing black men with their hands tied and cuffed behind their backs in the past is the white police force in uniform, with "GUNS" around their waste killing black men and women in broad daylight with crowds of black and white people watching. The police have no remorse or feelings about killing black people in 2020 than they did on slave ships during the transatlantic slave trade. The slave ships are the captured black men and women first introduction to rape and naming the slaves before sale at the end of the several month voyage. The slave ship captains and shipmates immediately separated the men and women so that they could have their way and their picks of any female that they saw and wanted.

From the seventh through the nineteenth dynasty the Portuguese took black slaves which they brokered with African Kings through the slave trade which already existed in Africa due to war captives. They took these slaves to Brazil and immediately took the men to sugar cane plantations twenty to thirty miles away and kept them separated so that the white slave masters could breed with the African women and create a light skinned race of Africans to create a separation between light skin and dark skinned people which changed and assisted in the mental breakdown of a whole race of people. Even if a slave master allowed a black couple to marry, the white slave master had sex with the expected wife until he impregnated her first to further create a separation in the black family and taking the manhood away from the black man in his own home. They did the very same thing in all of the Islands to include Cuba. Brazil and Cuba are the largest conglomeration of black populations light skinned people on Earth and it was done with the intentions of separating and breaking the African slave. White slave owners created the one woman parent homes I America and created a male since of carelessness about his children in several homes. This is the reasons for black on black crime, there's no real punishment or care for blacks killing other blacks. It was easy to allow drugs to enter black neighborhoods to destroy the minds of young black men and women and as soon as they made enough money to purchase cars homes and other property, the police moved in and arrested them putting them in prisons and taking the valuables for themselves. We are at a grave disadvantage in America when it comes to numbers. Although there are over a billion Africans all over the world in America we comprise only forty something million people as compared to three hundred and four million whites. We are not interested in a race war as some racist whites suggest we know the consequences; we simply have to develop our own. During the fifty years immediately after slavery there were hundreds of inventions developed by blacks which are being used and earning billions of dollars for with families today, that is why Nixon wrote in his book the annialation of the Negro by sending drugs into the black neighborhoods and prevent it from the white neighborhoods. The problems created for blacks by whites will exist indefinitely. Jails and prisons were built primarily for black people, a few whites get caught in the nets after committing numerous crimes before being sent to prison. A young black woman "Briana Taylor" was killed this year also in her own home, sleeping in her own bed with such a thing given to the police as the "NO KNOCK LAW", police can break into a black person's home regardless to weather there are children in the home and shoot it up! As black people we were all trained to beware of the white police, they are the new KKK now and they do not have to hide their faces or wait for the night to come to kill blacks, never kill whites, they offer whites water and burgers after they kill blacks. The officials in law claim there is an ongoing investigation immediately after they kill a black person when everyone saw it up close. Before we had phone cameras white police killed the same as they do today, with no fear of being convicted.

My Grandfather told me many times that a white man would laugh and joke with you, befriend and pretend to legitimately and sincerely have valued feelings for you, but that same evening when he is around his friends he would call a slave over to him and as entertainment for his friends, tell you to lift up your chin, and hit you as hard as he could to show his ease of knocking you down. They did not think black people had feelings of pain or sadness as white people did so they will always treat us unfairly simply because they can. When white people owned us they truly had it made and make no mistake many of them feel that same way today. We cannot expect white teachers to teach our children right they don't think that we deserve anything after we ran off, and fought against them in the Civil war, they will never forget because it is being taught every day in the homes today. We were the money of the slave holder, they not only could sell you at will or borrow money against you.

Secret Obstacles

In 1860 right here in my own home State of South Carolina is where seventy percent of the slaves for South Carolina, North Carolina and Georgia were sold came through Charleston South

Carolina. In November of that year it was decided in our Capital building that the population of slaves in South Carolina was 57 to 60 percent. They were worth more than all of the banks in the Country, more than all of the trains, all of the oil, all of the stock markets. Wall street in New York is where the slave market was. New York life insurance company was the first company to write an insurance policy for runaway slaves. Worth more than all insurance companies and all industrial companies in this Country. New York wrote a $500.00 life insurance police on a runaway slaves and also wrote policies on slave ships! The African slave made so much money for slave owners through rice and cotton until South Carolina was the richest State in the world. Eighty percent of the cotton exported in the world came from the South. Slaves were worth more than all of their commodities "PUT TOGETHER". So you see why white mothers and fathers sent their sons to war, some racist today feel that they have an inherit right to own slaves and the old way of life, no black female could refuse sex to a white man and then they said after they raped them, "They love it". Love to have sex with a white man. I sold Insurance for New York life, Metropolitan and "Mutual of Omaha" and I know how Insurance Companies make money. The Civil war though is the only time all slaves stuck together for one cause, The white slave owners could not understand how completely the slaves fooled them, pretending to love them so much-"we sick massa". That is one of the very reasons why white police officers join the police force is to "kill black people". The house Negroes men and women took silverware and other items they wanted, they told the Union soldiers exactly where the guns and money was hidden. They set fire to houses. Barnes, cotton and set fires to let the Union know where the whites were hiding. When South Carolina and all of the other ten Southern Slave states succeeded from the Union they committed Treason, punishable by Hanging. They had to get off of their land and forfeit everything of value. The South was printing their own money they were so wealthy. There was a slave owner in Georgetown named Ward who owned 1200 slaves and the Middleton plantation in Charleston had 800 slaves, you talking about rich, a slave was worth 2,500 at 16 years old, he could be given a trade such as horse shoeing, saddle making, brick mason and carpentry and they also used them for breeding. The poor whites as most were could never afford a slave but they still want to own one today! My father was skilled as his father was in brick masonry, carpentry and farming so my great-grandfather bought his farm while working in Brittensneck South Carolina, that's another reason I was dead set on owning my own business, my Dad rode around with money in his pockets but us children did not have anything unless we sold things like I did without my dad knowing, eggs, we had over one hundred chickens and they laid eggs everywhere. One day while my friend Lee and I picked up soda bottles off of 501 highway, only way to go to Myrtle beach, the store owner told me that he would pay me five cents per egg while he was only paying me a penny per soda bottle. That very moment that very day I quit the soda bottle business and begun my egg selling business and made lots of money which I kept in a vegetable canning jar.

Racism Then And Now

In the fifties and sixties when I was growing up we often heard about the brutality to blacks from white farmers usually, we never had much interaction with the police, most of us who lived in rural areas did not get access to cars until eleventh and twelfth grade in high school. There was a young man who had quit school in my hometown of Rains and worked as a farm worker year round for this farmer, white of course, one Saturday the farmer's younger son, about the same age as Daniel and they seemed to be close friends as one can be with a white man. A few of the fellas were going to Myrtle beach and he asked Daniel to ride along to do the cooking on the grill. They all got to drinking and having fun after the cooking was done so the white man Billy told Daniel to come under the umbrella for a minute and that's when Daniel said right out of the blue and for no reason other than for Billy to show his friends some excitement, he took out his knife and cut Daniel three or four times in the face, just for fun! Daniel had to live out his life with that memory and the scars, continued to work for that same man until someone gave him a ride to New York in the middle of the night and that's the last time anyone in the South saw Daniel. Whites do not look upon blacks as equals but the same as it used to be, as property! A white police officer can ask you a question as calmly as you please, and you respond in any way to him seems disrespectful, his attitude changes three hundred and fifty degrees in a second, your black skin seems to aggravate and anger white police to the point of what he joined the force for, to kill blacks. As soon as Zimmerman, the civilian who killed Trevon Martin and did not get convicted I knew that there would be more to come, I didn't think though that the killings would be so many and so frequent. The main problem that racist whites have with blacks is that they cannot own and treat blacks as they did in slavery. They cannot deport African Americans and they feel that they do not need us anymore now that slavery is gone. Every other race can be sent back to their home land, Chinese can be deported back to China, same as the Japanese, Mexicans, any people who are not white can be deported. The solution to racist police is to instill fear such that we can be controlled somehow knowing that they cut all ties to Africa when they destroyed our History, ancestry and family. African Americans have family in every major Country as slaves and we do not know each other. It is a sad feeling to me when I think about all of the black people all over the world related to me and I do not know them, close family.

Remnants Of Slavery

During the horrible, dirty Atlantic slave trade beginning with the Portuguese, they stole some and bought some, they hired African slave catchers to catch and steel young African men, women, girls and boys and marched them for many miles to holding bins to buildings along the coast that they got permission from African Kings to build, let's make no mistake, the Africans were complicate in the slave selling business long before the whites ever came. When they got between 350 and 500 Africans they loaded them that had been held in hot un-ventilated holding cells onto the ships for sail for six to ten weeks sometimes. Packed in the hull of the ships with no windows for air ventilation. They had to defecate and pee right where they were chained all during the trip, right on people who were chained beneath them and under them. The stink was so horrible until many died and were simply thrown overboard for the sharks to eat' Those Africans who were not broken and brain washed, individuals who had dreams of a life of their own just as their ancestors had before them. Dreams of working in their own chosen professions and trades, raising their own families and expecting to grow old and die in their own homeland! When the trip was complete after the men and women were always separated because the white had planned all the time to breed by rape all of the women that they wanted, separating a set woman crew to be breeders their whole lives on the plantations. The Portuguese took all of the men twenty to thirty miles away to the sugar cane plantations in Brazil where they whipped and castrated the men by the millions! You see white men have always been seriously jealous of the black man's sex organs. The Africans were not allowed to cohabitate or live with the women unless the owner decided that the couple would be a good match for producing strong healthy slaves children. These human beings were placed in a completely new and different environment which was harsh to say the least. They were beaten often to get them completely broken, not allowed to look a white person in the eye or talk back, they were worked for twelve to fourteen hours per day, from can to can't see, daylight until darkness. I cannot understand until this day how any human being could enjoy treating other humans like they were. The white overseer was relentless; it was his job to treat the people that we can call slaves now instead of Africans. They give names of the owner's choosing, the slaves could not speak or understand the language so they were beaten and given jesters of movement when the overseer wanted them to go here or go there. The slave owners all along was to breed with the African women in order to create a light skinned Mongoloid race of people for him to own as if he were a God. The Brazilian people today almost all light skinned people which they treated a might better than the black Africans to create recension among the entire plantation's people. This practice was initiated all along the Islands into Cuba-Cuba is almost completely Mongoloid-light skinned.

Spain were the next to get involved in the massive slave trade and they had a superior mastery of the seas and oceans so they wound up starting wars with the Portuguese for the right to get their pick of the best grade in size and age of the slaves that's why they still have forts standing on the ports of Africa today, abandoned. England got into the slave trade next and became the biggest slave traders of them all until this day, Columbus was not looking for new lands when he got lost, he was looking for the best entry port on the coast of Africa to buy slaves for the Queen of England. The triangle which is described in European History is from England (British) to Africa on to Brazil with slaves, A family of Africans comprised of eight family members to include the two parents, would be taken from Brazil first to be traded or sold for sugar and other spices, perhaps two from the African family, and then onto Barbados which was used as a braking ground for the slaves to be broken into submission before they were taken onto England as subservient and obedient servants for the rest of their lives. England owned, had colonized Barbados as they do in all weaker and darker skinned countries. Let s explain this term "Colonize", when the colonization begins in all of the weaker Countries, America whips the people into submission and then indoctrinate the people with their religion, the religion which they have changed many passages of scripture to serve their purposes such as "the older shall serve the younger" and "slaves obey your masters, with the promise of a better life in the hereafter! God did purposely place any of his children in bondage to another. It is highly understood and realized today that the black Africans were the first born on Earth and Africa is the cradle of all civilization. The black African ruled the entire world for the first (5000) five thousand years. We were the first people to venture into China, Japan America although it was not called America at first. During the Antediluvian era, the five thousand years before the flood all of the people black and brown people, we did encounter the white people until after 1000 BC- in our Bible the new testament Romans in Mathew Mark, Luke and John! From Adam to the flood, time was 2,212 years, from the flood to Abraham was 912 years, from Abraham to Moses time was 430 years, from Moses to David was 510 years, from David to the Babylonian captivity was 500 years and from the Babylonian captivity to the incar nation of Jesus Christ time was 400 years, for a total of 5,500 years, the time that Adam was originally supposed to live-not die and go back with Jesus! The Chinese and Japanese had our first five books of the old testament Bible and that original Egyptian Bible which is and has always been in Africa does not have anything about slaves obey your masters or the older shall serve the younger, it was put in the Bible by King James to gain wealth with slavery. Money is the root of cause of all evil, that is what allows white people to steal and sell entire congregations of people. For that very reason I have family members all over the world in every white dominated country that had power and numbers! Family members that I will never know. I have no knowledge of my last name. Ninety percent of the world's seven point five (750,000,000,000) billion people are people of color. The power of the "gun" changed the world. It is still changing the world today, the white police do not kill anyone but black people except in completely rare and unavoidable cases. Today the whites are killing black people left and right, both women and men.

After England abolished slavery, after they had built great and massive mansions, France, Spain, Portugal, Greece, Germany all got their Countries Cities and towns built along with their treasuries established they got rid of the dirty business of slavery and didn't give the African free men and women not one dime, just booted them out of their cabins until the slaves realized that they had no preparations to survive in America without depending on the American whites. The land in American when the Africans came as slaves about sixty percent of the land was swamp and woods. The slaves cut down trees, dug up the stumps, drained the swamps and cleared the land in every state of America as it is today. They built the roads, bridges, buildings to include the "white house" named for white people, the poor white say to black people, go back where you came from, we did not come here by paying our fairs, but we should go back the best way that you can so that they can forget!!! The slavery process had such a demonstrative holding effect on people until Indians enslaved black people in Georgia and Oklahoma, the trail of teers was Andrew Jackson wanted their land even after the Indians copied all of the practices of the whites. They took the slaves to Oklahoma and the slaves walked away from the Indians, the white Americans started to finish up the extinguishing the land of all Indians, that is why the African black did not team up with the Indians to fight, they wanted to be treated continually like they were almost white.

There was a black slave in Sumter County named "April" a man, owned by a slave master names William Ellison. He had April trained as an apprentice, taught him to read and write, hired him out to do odd jobs for wages which he shared with April. April worked at the cotton gin where he learned to repair and sharpen the cotton gin blades, became very good at it. April earned enough money to buy his freedom and when his owner agreed he let April go. He had been allowed to travel all over the State of South Carolina so April liked Marion South Carolina so he moved there, Marion is my hometown, he bought a house and plantation from a Judge, bought several hundred acres of land and guest what? April changed his name to William Ellison, the name of his former slave master and guest what? He begun to buy and breed slaves! It is said that William Ellison treated his slaves worse than any white man which takes some during, he also sold infant girls, he had three or four big women that he used for breeders and he breed them like hogs, every two years those women had children. Now you don't have to guess this time, there was a boy that flunked the ninth grade and we caught him there, he became our, my classmate named WB. Ellison and you know what he became after he was released from the army he became a police officer in Marion County. No one ever had any idea who he was I just found out a year ago while during research! WB. Ellison was said to have gone to his doctor's office after having chest pains two years ago and the doctor let him sit in the waiting room until he died, right there in the doctor's office! In Marion SC.

Just this year 2020, February I took my 2004 Avalanche truck to precision tune auto on garners ferry rd. just three miles from my home, same place that I 've taken both of my vehicles the 2014 Chevy impala for the past two years or so just for oil changes, I have professional thirty plus years' experience you no to do serious or major repairs I do not allow a multiple purpose auto service to do anything that they recommend I do, they create computer errors on your vehicle to get your money and keep you coming back. Well this guy has always admired my truck and I know that he wanted to steel it, here's how they get you-they play with the computer and direct it to send bad signals to your control panel and charge you a phenomenal amount of money but never completely do the job correctly. The idea is that if they can get you to agree to let them start the job they got you, they charge you enough money so they think that you cannot pay it within seven days, the law states that can take your vehicle in court. They send you a court date within thirty days and if you can't come up with the total amount of money in court the Judge has no choice but to rule in the mechanic's favor. I ask the guy on written paper to change my oil and check my air conditioner, it was getting hot and cold after a little while it was already hot weather and I wanted it checked with the machine used to detect problems, the guy gave me a bill for $1254.00 and that he had already done the work, he was instructed to "check air flow", so I paid him and went directly down to the human affairs office and filed a complaint, filed a bad report on my computer at home for the survey they send you. The guy called me as I was leaving the human affairs office and asked me if he could resolve the matter before things went any father, I told him that I tried to talk to you before I left your shop and you were not interested in anything but the full amount of the money, no there's nothing that you can do at this point I will see you in court! I went directly to the magistrate's office and filed a complaint which cost me $80.00 court cost. On the day we were to appear before the Judge the manager didn't show up, the owner of about six or seven precision tunes in the Columbia area, a rich white boy came in with another of his store managers and he came to court wearing short pants and t-shirt. The judge was a black woman and as I sat there waiting for my case to be heard I saw several black men and women lose their vehicles for that very same reason, couldn't pay the overcharge bill repairs. When the judge called my case I had already gone to the library and looked up the cost of the simple plug that was needed to regulate my air flow in my truck from $24.00 to $34.00 and recommended cost to repair was not to exceed $50.00 to install. I printed out the actual plug sheet with several different types and none cost more than $34.00 and not more than $50.00 to install, he charged me $1254.00 and would not allow me to go to my bank along with my truck which was two blocks away to get more cash, he already had two of my bank cards on file and I was not going to allow him to open up the charges to my card and inflate the price even more. The cocky white owner got up and presented the actual paper that I submitted to the manager to check, he went on to say that Mr.

Graves told us to fix several things on his truck and here is some of the evidence right here! The Judge looked at the written work order that I had given the manager and looked up and said -It says right here sir "Check" not fix. He was used to filibustering in court you see that's all that he does, he has managers to operate all of his stores. The Judge looked at me and said Mr. Graves is there anything else that you would like to say before I pass Judgement-I said yes your Honor, I have never seen this man before in my life, he was not the manager of that store that day that I took my truck in ever and anything that he says is here-say, he didn't bring the actual mnager here today because he knows that I could have gotten him for perjury, he would have to lie just like this fellow is doing here right now! The Judge said I'm ordering you to pay Mr. Graves back all of the money except the $250.00 cost for replacing the air oscillator for his air conditioner. He shrugged his shoulders and mumbled something, he had never lost a case before most people do not know how to prepare a motion in court and many white men feel that a black man has any rights that he should respect. The Judge told the owner to sit down sir and she called her officer to arrest him. I won the case, the Judge ordered the man to pay me my money and to this day that man has not obeyed the Judge's order to pay. I filed a complaint with the Federal trade dept. in Washington DC. The remnants of slavery will always be with us the racist descendants of slave owners still believe that have an inherent God given right to own slaves and they want us back! The power over a whole people and free labor, never having to work is too much for them to give up. Even after England abolished slavery they went to India and tricked, bamboozled young Indian men and women onto ships to go and replace us in the fields as indentured slaves-slavery reinvented. Mahatma Ghandi was successful lawyer and he gave up his practice, went to prison for years in protest against the enslavement of his people. In America after abolishing slavery in 1808 a slave trader in Charleston South Carolina as late as 1859 was caught with a ship load of African slaves just before they docked, the smell of the ship was so terrible that it is said that you could smell it from five miles away! Oh, the precision tune still has not paid me my money back he is still defying a court order, the Federal trade commission gives him one year before they come after his license.

There was a runaway slave born in 1833 named CR. Patterson escaped in 1861 and joined the Union Army in the Civil War.

When the War was over he went to Greenfield Ohio and started a carriage maker business which he later became the first American owned automobile manufacturing company, he had fifteen employees and also begun making buses to include school bused and cross country. There were over fourteen million slaves taken to Brazil and they were the last Country to abolish slavery in 1898. The United States tried to Colonize Cuba and did for a while until Fidel Castro overthrew their President and when the US didn't want to trade with him Castro formed a partnership with Russia, Cuba is another Country that the American slave traders created a light skinned race.

CHAPTER NINE

Black Life in the South VS the North

From an early age black children are taught very specific tools to deal with the problems of racism in the South. We were not allowed to go inside the sandwich shops in Marion so whenever I wanted to buy a hotdog from the local sandwich shop downtown I had to go to the designated window on the side of the store. The sales clerks were polite and always shinned the fake smile so that you would feel good about coming back. The Hot dogs seemed to be the best thing, perfect with chilies and onions and warmed bun. My brothers and I cropped tobacco and picked cotton to help purchase our school clothing however, I always ordered my dress boots from the eighth grade through College, i was voted the best dressed male in school- I knew how to put my colors together. I pressed my own blue jeans with starch so that they had a perfect crease in them. When I reached the age of fourteen my friend Lee and I managed to get his older brother to take us to get our driving license and we both got them the first time the same day, I had been driving around our farm since I was nine years old and sometimes we drove short distances on 501 highway when it wasn't beach season with the terrible traffic flow all of the time. One Saturday my Mom asked me to drive her downtown to do some shopping, it was such that I was good at parallel parking. We were about four miles away from town and I realized that we were following a highway patrolman who was driving about forty five miles per hour in a fifty five mile per hour speed limit. I summarized that there would be nothing wrong with passing the patrolman when it was within the law. Wouldn't you know it, the Patrolman immediately pulled me over and approached the car, I asked? Is there something wrong officer? You passed me with the yellow line in your lane.

I looked back behind me and realized that he had waited following me until I reached the yellow line before he pulled me over. I looked at Mom with my facial expression as to knowing that there was no need for me to say anything else, the Police were always right so I said yes sir and proceeded to just look out over the stirring wheel. The ticket was $15.00 but Mom didn't mind paying it she was proud of my courage and my courtesy. I never had another encounter with the Police until I was a grown man in my twenties, in fact we never saw the Police unless they were just cruising down the busy 501 highway. I had relatives though living in Baltimore, Washington and New York who had totally different experiences with the police. In the Northern Cities, there is concrete everywhere, there is no such thing as a dirt road. In the North the police not only frame you by putting a gun in your possession they arrest the blacks without provocation all of the time. White people mostly have absolutely no idea what black people experience with police. Black bodies in prison and county jails pay the salaries of all Judges, all Lawyers, Attorney Generals and police officers, all prison guards and court officials. All probation employees and halfway houses. The police do not arrest white people unless it is absolutely necessary and cannot be avoided I was the Assistant principal at DJJ for many years and I knew all Judges in my State by name. The police will find doup-drugs on a black person who has never seen drugs up close and wind up doing time so that the State can collect the $27,000 every January 1st And July 1st every year. On January 6'st everyone in this Country saw the infamous day that explains everything that I mentioned previously about the police being formed in 1641 expressly for black people.

The white racist groups bombarded the Capital building in Washington DC to kill the white Vice President and Nancy Pelosi, Chairwoman of the Democratic party along with anyone else that they could find. The police Chief in Washington DC Knew in advance that they were coming so they did not arm themselves properly to contain the violence. No extra officers were called until the Capital building has been totally taken over by the white "MOB" instigated by the US President of the United States of America. The Police Chief called the National Guard but when they saw on TV that the intruders were white the National guard and all other Military forces called just refused to come-they were not going to arrest the white people, CIA AND FBI included. Seven people died and hundreds were injured but hardly any arrest were made until the next day or so, if they had been black every police officer within miles would have come to get their chance to kill a black person. It is a known fact that some white police officers join the force to kill black men women and children. We saw on National TV the white police officer held his knee on "George Floyd's neck until he was dead. Without any thought of the fact that he was killing a black father, husband and Mother's son! It cannot be explained to any black person the fate when you encounter a white police officer. I looked in horror as I saw on TV the white officer shoots the black man in Charleston South Carolina nine times in the back as he was un-armed and running away-the officer then calmly walked over to his body while talking on his to way radio, "tazor tazor tazor" to indicate that the black man was resisting, he then dropped his tazor on the black man's body to cover the fact that he had just murdered the man and that he was supposedly trying to take the officers tazor. Someone was looking and filming the entire incident!

Contrasting the North and South, we do not express the letter (R) in our speech we simply say (dis) and dat instead of this and that there. We readily acknowledge the "shotguns) hanging in the rear window of trucks, nigger getters. Trucks and cars with the dull gray color, red as well. We have been trained from an early age to recognize the whites who carry within themselves hatred and bigotry. We recognize that we pay higher interest rates on homes, cars and any other property that you pay on time to ownership. Credit beacon scores did not exist until 1946 when the GI's came home from world war two and started buying new homes in white neighborhoods. The only jobs that we could get in the South were farm work jobs.in the North there were lots of jobs because of the industry that has developed. I graduated from high school in 1966 and the first job I had at the age of 17 was at a company called "Coats board and Carton company in Patterson New Jersey, my job was to feed the flattened card board soap container into a machine which shaped and sealed it into the box that tide and other clothes washing powder that you see in stores today, although many are in plastic bottle containers today. I was treated fairly good as well as in the South the Whites had no choice but to treat you nice because the only people in the South for a very long time were just blacks and whites, the whites had to have hired hands in the summer and fall to gather their crops and those hands were blacks. We lived 37 miles from Myrtle Beach and during the Summer that's where we went- but we had to drive past Myrtle beach to Atlantic beach, the black beach about five miles past Myrtle beach, it wasn't until the late sixties before we could go to Myrtle beach after the passing of the Civil rights act of 1964.

Patterson New Jersey was predominantly black and the only restaurants were the Kentucky fried chicken, Maryland fried chicken and a McDonalds, today both the Kentucky fried and Maryland chicken has closed only the McDonalds still exist. After the Summer was over I moved to the Bronx New York what a difference. The streets were filled all day and all night with multi-racial people, people from all over the world were living in New York and they all get along. Within a couple of weeks after I arrived in New York and received my first pay check and took a young lady out for drinks at a local night club, now the first thing that she asks me was to give her ten dollars to pay her baby sitter while we were out, I had no idea that she had a child and I only received $87.00 dollars from my paycheck. The next thing that she asks me was to take a cab and that cost me almost $20.00, trust me, I was ready to take her back home before we ever went inside the club. I was planning to save money to buy me a car and within five years buy a house. When we left the club I told her that we would have to take the subway and guest what? She took out a crisp $50.00-dollar bill and gave it to me to pay for a cab. I said to myself, the mentality of this city was way beyond me, New

York would not be the place for me to live for very long and it just so happened that I received a call from my high school principal encouraging me to Go to College and avoid the trip to Vietnam. I did not develop male friendships in New York they seemed to think all southerners were stupid and easy pickens. No one seemed to ever go to Church in this city not at all like the South, in South Carolina we went to Sunday school and regular service every Sunday and sometimes on Friday nights. There was absolutely no way to not go to Church on Sunday Mom would come into me and my brothers room with a broom!

I remember when we got the first black police officer in my hometown and he was not allowed to arrest any white people, just blacks just like the white police officers. I went home for Christmas that year in 1966 and on Christmas eve I drove my Mom's car to the club that we called "moon Light" it was always packed but before me and my friend Lee who was following me, the one black police officer that we had was sitting back in a speed trap and as soon as we past him he pulled out and turned on the blue lights on Lee first then past him and drove up to my window and yelled "follow me". He led us directly to the County jail without saying anything, I was glad because I had a fifth of Cutty Sark scotch under my driver's seat but not opened. We walked inside and there was a fat white officer sitting behind the desk, the black officer asked us for $25.00 a piece and he would let us go, I only had about $60.00 and it was Christmas eve, Lee said adamantly, I ain't got no money and he stuck with it until I told the officer that I only had $15.00 more dollars-will you let us go for that, alright get out of here. When I walked out to my car I asked Lee? Boy what do think that you were doing in there defying the law don, t you know that they kill black people in jail and say that they hanged themselves. He said that that is what that black officer did all of the time they don't allow him to write any tickets he just rob black people and take what the white police chief gives him, that's how he earns his salary he was not smart enough to write tickets they want hire any black intelligent officer, you're kidding, now I felt like these Southern white people were thinking over my head I have a lot to learn. After living in two Northern cities I realized for the first time in my life that Marion-my hometown had absolutely nothing in it except one Kentucky fried chicken and one McDonalds and Hardees!

During my College years I spent some summers in Baltimore Maryland, Baltimore is the last Southern State and it is much more to my liking than any other State. I spent a year in Baltimore while I was under some great ambiguity concerning having to go to Vietnam. I found Baltimore was pleasant and in 1969 money was flowing freely, anyone who wanted a job could get one that would pay you well. I got a job with one of my brothers at the Baltimore Smeltering and refining company, they paid me $350.00 per week and double time if you worked overtime. This company was smeltering Gold, Nickel and copper products. Shortly after I started to work there the supervisor asked me to be the person who could take the lunch orders for a huge number of employees since I had some College learning experience. Writing down the orders and keeping an accurate account of the money to pay for orders and return change however most men just gave me whatever change was left. It was a good and rewarding deal for me. I met a girl whom I will call Ros and a good male friend that I hung out with called Shepp, many years later when I was forty years old I moved back to Baltimore and stayed four years. I taught Shepp how to drive and we had a lot of fun I miss him.

African American Churches

Even before slavery was abolished the black slaves begun building and establishing Churches all over this Country. Soon after they begun building Colleges Fisk in Tennessee was the first in the South. The Churches were the life blood of the African American in matters of not only survival but uplifting the black race. Many Churches were burned the same as it is in modern times, white supremacist are adamantly worried about the blacks rising. The numbers of white Americans has a low Melanin count in their blood, blacks have the highest on Earth. The Churches taught within their walls reading writing and arithmetic. Matters concerning building and construction and etc. The compiling of money and feeding the hungry and burying the dead to assist poor families. I am the founder of ON TTRACC BIBLE BUSINESS COLLEGE-in 2004 lead by the spirit into my purpose. The College offers Degrees in African and African American History and culture to include Languages, job creation-work from home also. Education-teachers and self-employment. In Timbuckto and Sudan in Africa, a black King established great institutions of higher learning the same as Egypt. King Mansa Musa was the richest King that ever lived. He had so much Gold it was recorded as being over $450, 000,000,000, Billion dollars in today's calculations. Much more than John d. Rockefeller at $ 204,000,000,000 Billion dollars, Henry Ford at $200,000,000 Billion dollars and all others as well. Mansa Musa had so much gold until he took 200 camels loaded down with gold to Egypt and literally gave it away to commoners and the government of the black king in Egypt He gave so much until he disrupted the Egyptian economy for twelve years!

Mansa Musa caused an imbalance in Egypt's GNP such that Egypt did not recover for twelve years, he also gave gold mines to King Solomon in Jerusalem and made Solomon the richest king to ever live in Jerusalem. Mansa Musa sent out over two hundred ships during his lifetime all over the world to make new discoveries in lands and to broaden his territories. He sent several ships to the land that we call America today, The Piquot Indians (Black) settled in America a thousand years before Columbus re-discovered America! In 1637 just 17 years before the first slaves were taken to Virginia as endentured cervatude, (7 years) of slavery and then they became free and went back to Charleston South Carolina. The first Thanksgiving celebration that we were taught in schools all over America where we saw the Indians giving the whites food and teaching them how to farm and survive the whites had Guns since 1350 and those Indians were Black Piquot tribe which were Slaughtered by the Pilgrims and took some of the Blacks back to England as Slaves! When saw the cowboys on TV killing Indians we were rooting for the cowboys, not knowing that those Indians were the first to settle in this Country and that they were "Black". The writer James Baldwin wrote about the same thing in one of his books. The white Supremacist are screaming take their Country back and make the Country great again- meaning slavery. There is so much Black History that's never taught in any schools until it is silly. We will get the job done in time it is just a matter of waiting to get funding for our Administration Building. All things come to the light and equality is inevitable. The Piquot Indian Tribes are living and thriving in the west, California and some in Florida different from the black Seminoles comprised of black runaway slaves and others.

ON TTRACC BIBLE BUSINESS COLLEGE was founded by yours truly in 2004 and is inception is based on the track that God created for every individual on Earth to fulfill the purpose of one's life and God 's plan for his world. I am a Minister and Historian and part of my purpose is to educate our people from Junior high school thru College. Absolutely no one is going to teach our people how to build and manage their own Businesses, it Is counter intuitive for black people to become equal to white people, the people who brought us here to work for free forever! The address 11-12 wall street is the "Stock market" address, this is the address of the first and largest slave market in the world, NYSE. The following is a listing of the richest and most powerful people in the history of the world.

> John D. Rockefeller-life earnings and acquisitions-$367 Billion dollars.
>
> Henry Ford-$202 Billion dollars
>
> Carnelius Vanderbilt $200 Billion dollars
>
> Gaddafi, Libbia Africa-$200 Billion
>
> Old age Jakob Fugger Roman Banker in 1100BC $277 Billion

Usman Kahn-India $200 Billion

Tzar Nicholas Russia-$300 Billion

Kahn the Mongolian $100 trillion plus 1,000,000 sq. miles of land.

Kahn the only ruler who redistributed the wealth to his subjects.

Emperor ShenZang of China, $30 trillion

1067BC in Akbar Japan $21 Trillion

Emperor Augustus-$5 Trillion

King Solomon $ 2 Billion and also uncountable wealth from salt and Land

"NOW" The black King Mansa Musa from Timbutu and Sudan $415 Trillion also owned 50% of the world's Gold and 50% of the world's salt, he controlled the entire salt trade which was worth more than Gold at that time.

In 1859 the Suez Canal-the manmade waterway was constructed in the attempt separate and cut out Jerusalem, Somaria, Palestine (new developed name for Caanan) cut out from North Africa, it's now called the "Middle East"

It is an exciting time 2021 to help develop the African and African American College, the Address is

ED Graves-ON TTRACC BIBLE BUSINESS COLLEGE 7645 GARNERS FERRY RD. BOX 1015C COLUMBIA SC. 29209

Donations can be check or money order and I will place your name on a calendar wall in the lobby of the Administration building. 501-c-3 certification for tax deductions.

I was in Baltimore MD from 1991 until 1995 managing a sales office for Metropolitan Life and Brokered for a few others. There was a Lady friend that I called HB who was a great help to me in those years, the attitude of the people in Baltimore is remorseful in that the living conditions has greatly diminished since i first spent the 1969 and 70 there. Everyone was working and making money, driving nice cars and owned their homes. Now the streets are loitered with furniture thrown out because folks cannot pay notes and rent. The steel mills and other industries have closed down and moved out of the Country. The streets are filled with homeless people who cannot find a job. White America owns the jobs in America and they can do what they want with them, God bless the child who has his own. We cannot expect anyone to keep giving to us and we are too talented to keep waiting for things to come to us on a platter. There is no feeling equal to turning the key to your own home and what is greater is to turn the key to your own business. When you own your own Cars and home the feeling hard to explain, it is a freedom that few have felt. When you work for someone else your time with your family is not your own when you have to think about having to go to bed at a certain hour every night so that you can get up at a certain hour to go to someone else's company job. Not realizing that the owner can cut your life cord at any time specifically after you reach the age of 38 and 39 having spent your best years there. You have absolutely no control over when you will get cut.

CHAPTER TEN

Africa And Its Resources

Africa is the second largest continent to China due to genocide and exploitation, second in the world. God began his world here with "Adam" and for the first two hundred years it is suggested that all of Adam's children and descendants were pure "Black skinned" they traveled and explored the entire planet with great success. God put everything that man would need for eternity in the garden and throughout Africa. Some of the precious resources and commodities are as follows Diamonds, sugar, salt, Gold, iron, Cobalt, uranium, copper, "Bauxite" is the material used in all batteries, all cell phones etc. silver petroleum, cocoa and cocoa beans, all sorts of tropical fruits. Many of these items are being terribly exploited simply because the wealthy Kings and corrupt Governments make Nefarious deals for themselves, the same way that it has been done for centuries to include the selling of slaves. They do nothing for their economies.

The Ten Richest Kings In Africa

1. King Mohamad vi of Morocco-$2 Billion
2. OBA Fredrick Obateru Akinrutan of Nigeria, a very large Country-$300 Million
3. The Sultan Sa-adu AbuBakar III of Sokoto-$100 Million
4. King Mswati 111 of Swaziland-$50 Million

5. Obi Nnaemeka Afred Ugochukwu Achebe of Onitsha-Nigeria $50 Million

6. Oba Rilwan Akiolu of Lagos Negeria-$40 Million

7. Otumfuo Osei TuTu of Ashanti Ghana-$40 Million

8. Togbe Afreda xiv of Ghana State-$30 Million

9. King Zwelihni of Zulu S. Africa-$6 Million

10. Osagyefuo Nana Amoati Ofori of Akyen Abukwa-Ghana-$28 Million

America and other world countries include the following:

1. John D. Rockefeller-$367 Billion

2. Henry Ford-$202 Billion

3. Carnelelius Vanderbilt-$ 200 Billion

4. Gaddafi-Libia-Africa $200 Billion

5. OLD age-Jakob Fugger, Russian Banker 1100 BC $277 Billion

6. Osman Kahn India $230 Billion

7. Tzar Nicholas Russia-$300 Billion

8. Kahn $100 Billion plus 12 million square miles of land, he is the only ruler who redistributed the wealth to his subjects.

9. Emperor Shen Zang, China-$30 Trillion

10. 1067 BC- Akbar of Japan $21 Trillion

11. Emperor Augustus- $5 Trillion

12. King Solomon $2 Billion, however he controlled 50% percent of the salt trade which was un countable because it was worth more than Gold at that Time, The Queen of Sheba Gave him $6 Million in Gold, silk and every

King in all surrounding territories gave wealth of Horses and all sorts of exotic animals continuously throughout his 40-year reign. King Solomon would have parades at a whim capriciously to display some of his wealth, He had 40 thousand horses and taken from 1st Kings, the provisions for his table for one day was 30 measures of fine flour, and three score measures of meal 300 bushels-600 bushels, 10 fat oxen and twenty oxen out of pastures, 100 sheep, beside harts (Small deer) roebucks and fallow deer, fatted foul. Solomon had forty thousand stalls of horses for his chariots and 12 thousand horsemen and officers who provided food for the king and for all who came to Solomon's table each man his month in the year, Solomon lacked nothing, he ruled the lands all around unto the steps of Egypt. God gave Solomon wisdom and understand beyond any human. Solomon spoke three thousand proverbs

FOOTNOTE: 1st Kings previous page, King Solomon ruled for forty years and there was no hunger and no "War" even his servants wore Golden Bracelets, rings and ankle bracelets. Solomon was only 15 Years when his father King David died. David left Solomon the instructions and the financial monies to build God's temple in Jerusalem, he also left 139 wives and Solomon took them into his fold. The custom in those days was that a king should take as many wives into his house, which was about 25,000 acres of land. Egypt was the world power at that time so King Solomon married the daughter of the king of Egypt, creating his first ally. The young King Solomon went out into the desert to commune with God before he ever sat on the seat of the King! Some things are too powerful for God to speak to mankind directly so when Solomon went to sleep by his campfire God ask him what would you ask of me? Solomon said that he was only a kid and he did not know how to go out or come in, please grant me an understanding heart and the wisdom to rule over his people which was of a great number-over a Million. God said -since you didn't ask for riches, or a long life nor the life of his enemies, he would grant him the understanding heart such that it would be as vast as the sand on a seashore and the "Wisdom" would be greater than any King or man who ever lived or will live after him. I will give you riches greater than any King who ever lived and will ever live after you. When Solomon went to his court the next day he sat on the throne for the first time and his first case was concerning the two prostitutes who had the dead child and the other live child which both women were claiming. Solomon asked for a sword from his court officer and threatened to cut the child in half and give both half of the severed child, but before he touched the child with the sword- the true mother threw herself over the child and said to The King, Give the child to her, I would wish above all things that my child lives. King Solomon took the live child and gave him to her saying, this is the true mother. Immediately after that case was settled King Solomon wrote out a "Royal decree" stating that because my father King David had wars and rumors of wars it left thousands of widows who were being brutalized, sexually abused and if those women didn't have a male child they could not own land or any property so they were left in a very precarious position! The Decree (LAW) stated that every widow in his territory will be given an invitation to be his "Concubines" and that he would build each one their own house and feed and take of all that came, some he would marry. Solomon wound up with 300 wives and seven hundred concubines, 1,000. this is the factor that annoyed me many years when a 5-year-old child heard this story they always said that King Solomon was "Stupid" The wisest King that ever lived was stupid and had since enough to know that the only place that one can get wisdom is from "GOD himself" old and gray hair only gives you experience, you know what to do and what not to do because you have seen and done it before! King Solomon ordered hundreds of his officers to begin building the houses for his concubines. The good fortune did not end there for the women, if they could get pregnant from the King perhaps it would be a son whom the King would show and give favor, perhaps even name him as a successor to the throne. Following day King Solomon went to mount Gibeon and sacrificed 1,000 young bullops, your male calf. Everyone from miles around would come to ask advice and questions about what and when to plant fields of crops and any other thing that you can think of, how to solve disputes with neighbors, anything that you could think of to ask the King he could answer it and they all brought valuable gifts for the King!

The time came King Solomon took on the task of building the Temple for God that his father King David told and gave him the instructions from God. King David was on the roof top one day because Uriah the Hittite warrior, greatest fighters in the land, The Hittites from central Africa came and defeated the Egyptians during the 25th Dynasty and ruled under their Pharaoh for many years That is why King Solomon married the Egyptian King's daughter to keep the peace, as he did all over his territories and Kings that he ruled over. Bath-Sheba was from Ethiopia, the people who has the most beautiful golden brown skin in the world. She had her two hand maidens assisting her in taking the special monthly bath that all women take after their cycle. King David saw the water flowing in and out until it became clear and David became so excited until he could not take it so he sent for her that very day, no one can refuse or say no to a King! That is how she became known as "Bath Sheba" and they had one son who died and the next son was "Solomon". King David was also brown skinned he was the eight son of Jesse. Solomon appointed 12 officers-12 is the number to establish governments, such as the 12 disciples of Jesus. Those 12 were given the order to supply the Kings food for one month each out of the year for all wives, concubines and all guests who wanted to come. The day came when King Solomon sent out the order (Decree) for all masons and carpenters in Jerusalem to come to his court. Solomon laid out and explained that no metal was to be used in building the temple except "Gold". All masons, helpers and carpenters were to work only 30 days and take off 60 days with pay to take care of their homes and farms. Solomon was a master at everything and his workers like everyone else loved King Solomon! It took seven years which was Solomon" s plan, seven is the number of completion and perfection!

Bath Sheba, David's wife from Ethiopia came from a line of Queens also "Queen Candace's), She sent for The Queen of Sheba to meet her son the famous King Solomon. It took six months to travel the 1400 hundred mile trip by caravan of over 300 guards and hunters with all the comforts of home. King Solomon convinced her to marry him and she stayed with him in Jerusalem for one year and they produced a son Named Meneleke who became King of Ethiopia, the New for Canaan. She was the only wife that he loved all of his life and he traveled to Ethiopia frequently throughout his days.

Ethiopia is located on the horn of Africa and has some beautiful scenery, this is the promise land that God told Abraham to leave his home Country of Iraq and go to live. Ethiopia is the only African Country that was never captured and colonized. The Ethiopians defeated the Spanish, French and romans in battle. Africa has 54 Countries on its Continent and Ethiopia has its own airplane production companies and pilots. Africa has a problem of too many languages spoken-over 500 different dialects spoken-perhaps this would help elevate the corruption of Governments which are leaning too heavily on the Economies.

Many African Americans cannot afford to go back home to visit and what else is strange is that we have to have a passport to go home after we were brought here against our will. It has never been easy for an African American living in America, there's always the police to look out for with high interest rates to pay on everything. America is the only successful multi-racial Country in the world, there are 241 recognized countries with an established Government in place, Ninety percent of those Countries are inhabited by people of Color.

ON TTRACC BBC addresses
our "HOLY BIBLE"

The Ancient Egyptian text contains the history of Africa, the beginning of all civilization beginning with ADAM. All characters in our real Bible beginning with Geneses through Malachi contains all Bible History and "All People contained therein are "Black and Brown "people, we did not engage with white people until the New Testament with the Romans in Mathew, Mark, Luke and John! Egypt was always the learning Capital of the World and everyone from Greece beginning in 8,000 BC, Egypt History begun in 5,000 BC, Before Christ. All other Countries Came to Egypt to study medicine, mathematics, Astronomy etc. The Capital of Egypt was "Memphis" where the world's library kept all African History from the beginning of the world. Alexander the Great concurred Egypt and was so amazed with all of the building constructions he did not want any other white nations to believe that this all was done by "Black people" He burned the Library and everything that depicts African Knowledge. It was later that "Napoleon who came later to concur Egypt and directed his "Cannons" on the "Spinx" to destroy the shape of the nose of a black King. While the Romans were enthused by the Egyptian Bible and the story of the Life of "Jesus Christ" while they ruled they changed all of the "Black people" and replaced them with white people! SO Jesus became white under white Roman occupation of Egypt! IN 1526 the first writings and recordings of "Slavery" and white Supremacy indicates that the most certain procedure in subjugating a people is to create a religion showing a white God and all powers on Earth was in the hands of all white people-slave owners and common citizens as well! Africans were always very spiritual people so it was relatively easy to indoctrinate African Slaves to white supremacy! The Holy Bible was changed 7 times through translations. The African slaves realized before they ever left the African shores in the holding cells that slave traders built to humiliate the African slaves that they had bought and stolen. Slaves realized that they had absolutely no control over their bodies and their lives, their children's lives!

In 1611 when King James of England was King he ordered and hired 50 scribes, specialist in hand writing that they had been taught from the age of three years old. It is the Holy Bible that we use all over the world today. In breaking a new slave, they were made to watch slaves whipped within an inch of life, a young pregnant black girl was tied to a tree the slave driver would cut the baby out of her stomach and then stomped on the head until death. That's the first day on to plantation!

Many black preachers know the truth about our Bible but the ramifications from preaching are too great, too many black are still too deeply under the teachings of "White Supremacy". This is an indoctrination that will take time even today. Every black family had a picture of a white "Jesus "on their living room wall in their parents' home. Even though the Africans could sense the truth in their spirits it was still fearful to try and think differently. Brainwashing is a very powerful and false teaching that many Countries use in Counter intelligence to indoctrinate spies. We've often and frequently even today experience the Tactics of Russia's indoctrination of people that we know.

In 1808 England outlawed and ended the slave trade in that Country but the wealth accumulated was tremendous. The slave trade still continued illegally In 1859 there was an attempt to cut out parts of Africa by constructing the "Suez Canal" the man made waterway to separate Africa from Asia, by cutting out Jerusalem, Sommaria, Palestine of Israel and develop a new man made Canaan today is called "the Middle East" all cut out of North Africa.

In 1884 There was what was known as the Berlin Conference in Europe and subsequently the division of Africa. There were 13 countries envolved to include the United States, Austria, Hungary, Belgium, Denmark, France Germany, Italy, The Netherlands, Ottoman Empire, Portugal, Russia, Spain Sweden, Norway, and the United Kingdom. All of these drew a Map of the Continent of Africa and marked of which parts they would take and Colonize and enslave the Africans on their own Lands. They stripped all Countries of their Natural Resources-Diamonds Golds etc. and left the citizens of Africa Hopeless. Today most of the inhabitants in Africa are living in poverty, having to go down three and four hundred feet underground to dig for Gold and diamonds for three and four dollars making White people extremely richer! But some black people manage to thrive wherever they are. These are the richest Kings in Africa.

1. King Mohammed vi of Morocco—$2 Billion dollars
2. OBA Fredrick Obateru Akinrutan – Nigeria $300 Million

3. Sultan Sa-adu Aburakar 111 of Sokoto $100 Millionaire
4. King Mswati 111 of Swaziland $ 50 Million
5. Obi Nnaemeka Afred Ugochukwu Achebe of Onitsha-Nigeria $50 Million
6. Oba Rilwan Akiolu of Lagos Nigeria $ 40 Million
7. Otumfuo Oswei TUTU of Ashanti Ghana $ 40 Million
8. Togbe Afrde xiv of State Ghana $ 30 Million
9. King Zwelithni of ZULU S. Africa $ 6 Million

Richest Blacks In The World

1. Kanya West $ 3 Billion
2. Oprah Windfrey $2.7 Billion
3. Strive Nasilywa 2.4 Billion
4. Patrice Motsepe $ 2.3 Billion
5. Michael Jordan $ 2.1 Billion
6. Folorunnsho AlaKija $ 1.1 Billion
7. Jay-Z $ 1 Billion
8. Tyler Perry $ 1 Billion
9. The richest black businessman in the World Aliko Dangote $ 13.5 "Billion"

One day the rich King "Solomon" after he had finished his court proceedings of answering all of the questions that other kings had traveled to ask questions about various things related to ruling and thier ruling and their family lives as well the King decided to tell them a "Joke". Everyone in Africa is familiar with deserts so he asks? "How do you find running water in a dry desert" everyone also knows that there is no running water in a dry desert to find, so after about ten minutes no one had any idea how to answer this question and neither would I, King Solomon said, take any team of horses or one even, and you "run the horse until him "sweat"-water running down the sides of the horses! Solomon had wisdom even in his Jesting. He had had wisdom in Medicine and he had the ability to communicate to with every animal that walketh upon the Earth, every creature that swimmeth in the Sea, Every creature that creapeth beneath the Earth and every foul that fly in the air! Adam Named every creature that God made but it was Solomon who separated the foul- Pigeons from birds, hawks from Eagles, Chickens from Turkeys etc. all Kings who visited king Solomon for whatever the reason, they brought him gifts, and what gift do you bring to the richest king in the land-" Young Virgins". King Solomon said when he was just reflecting one day, a man can have fleets of ships, thousands of horses and chariots 100 children and Gold and silver beyond measure- But if that man cannot taste his riches and he cannot "Sleep" he is the poorest man on Earth!

Jeff Bezos the owner and founder of Amazon and the Washington Post newspaper, he is currently the richest man in America with $179 Billion dollars followed by Bill Gates with $111 Billion, Mark Zukerberg $ 85 Billion and Warren Buffet with $73 Billion dollars. Comparatively black richest include Kanya West with $ 3.1 Billion, Oprah Windfrey, $2.7 Billion, Michael Jordan $2.1 Billion and Jay-Z $1 Billion, Tyler Perry $ 1 Billion dollars.

The African richest businessmen are Istrive Masilyiwa $2.4 Billion $ Folorunsho AlaKija $1.1 Billion dollars. The" richest man in the world" is African businessman "Aliko Dangote "$ 13.5 Billion dollars".

However, in our past History the "richest man who ever lived is the African King of Mali and Timbucktu "Mansa Musa", his total worth was $ 457 Billion Dollars and in today's worth is $ 6 Trillion dollars. He acquired 24 Countries, build Universities, and Synagogues that still stand today. He became King in 1320 BC. His trip to Mecca accommodated over 60,000 people to include military, guards, slaves and all the comforts of the rich King- he had hundred, cooks. He carried 200 camels loaded down with 300 pounds of "Gold" he gave away so much Gold until it devalued Gold and other monetary commodities for 12 years. In my opinion massive wealth above a few million would be burdensome for me because we are supposed to give most of your acquired wealth before we die. Absolutely no money is ever going to leave the Earth, it all belongs to God.

King David left 139 wives when he died and considerable wealth insuring that his son King Solomon would inherit great "Wealth".

King David was an old man and his health was failing him, His wife Bath Sheba ask him if she could get him a young Virgin perhaps she could revive his health. David agreed and she told Solomon to find the young beautiful Ab-i-Shag the "Shulamite" and bring her into the Palace to be a nurse and comfort to David. The Shulamites were very "dark" skinned Africans with velvety looking skin. Ab-i-shag was trained by her father in medicinal herbs from plants found in the forest as many Africans use today. David was too far gone so he died in about two weeks. Abraham was the father of the Israelites, he was 70 years old when God called him and instructed him to leave his home and go to a land that he would show him to be the promise land for God's people, "CAANAN" The old name for Ethiopia. Throughout our Old Testament Bible Ethiopia was always the seeking place to be for God's people. Out of Abraham came Isaac, Ismael the first born, Esau and Jacob from Isaac and it is Jacob's line that we follow-12 sons of Jacob-Joseph and Benjamin from Rachel and Joseph Jacob's favorite son was sold into slavery by his Jealous brothers. He became the famous Governor -ruler who saved not only Egypt from the seven year drought but the surrounding Cities as well. Benjamin, the younger brother of Joseph is not known for anything other than God chose his tribe to establish the Kings-First Saul and Saul was disobedient and God took his throne away, however the young David Killed the 9'9" brown skinned "Goliath". Goliath had a 52" breast from shoulder to shoulder, had four brothers and one was 13' feet tall, Goliath was the meanest and most skilled fighter but he was not the largest. When Saul realized that God was going to take his crown and Power away and give it to David he tried viciously to kill him. David found refuge in living with the Philistines for two years before he went into Jerusalem to take his place as King!

IN Africa 711 BC the "Moors" Came out of The western part of Africa and went into "Spain" and concurred it and ruled Spain for 700 years, the "Gun" was not made until 1350 AD. The Moors built beautiful buildings and Churches-paved the streets and developed flowing of water into the Cities of Spain.

CHAPTER ELEVEN

Slavery's Hang-Overs

Being an African American living in America my thoughts are my constant friendships, some good and some very bad! Each time that I re-visit the stories told to me and the memories that I've developed with my own experiences, the fact that everyone who sees me- my general appearance and skin color that can only come from "Africa", the whites as well as all other Nationalities know that my people were slaves for 400 years and built this Country that we are very seriously hated! What bothers me is that knowing that we worked for free and everything that comes with Slavery, leaves me to understand that some white people are not satisfied they want to have slaves again forever.

The "Palenque" Africans in South America between Brazil and Mexico were the first Africans to gain their freedom in War before Haiti. They have developed their own language and economy without the interference and influence of white people! When other Nationalities look upon me they have to see great people like Jack Johnson and Joe Louis, Aretha Frankin, Wilt Chamberlain and Kareem, Michael Jordan and Serena and Venus Williams and many other scholars, writers and actors- many others. We face discriminations of all kinds the moment we step outside our doors each morning and still we overcome. My first and last name are my first reminders of captivity, my family has been in America since 1630 along with the Pequot Africans that were slaughtered. In our Bible it is written in Deuteronomy 28-68.

That we would be brought to America in "Ships" but we also would be set apart and on high. Meta-physics describes our movements will be done with the Mind! Our purpose is to do like the drop of water which is cast too far inland from the Ocean which is the God of drops of water that have since enough to always go back to its God.

Blacks Who Owned Slaves

There was a young man from my own hometown who got left back in the Ninth grade at my high school and wound up in my class but no one knew the history of his great grandfather who owned and breaded slaves. It is said that this man was worse than most white slave owners-he bread women and sold their newborn babies as a normal practice for financial gain. I was during my usual research and came across his name and background and where his plantation was. He was the fourth richest slave owner in South Carolina. I was shocked, couldn't believe that it was possible but it all checked out! My mind will not allow me to consider such as thing as real. I've faced racism in employment and at the time I thought that you would always be rewarded for being good but I was awakened indeed! There was absolutely no thought given to my career or my family it was all about having someone white to replace me. They quickly realized that not just anyone could come in and work at the level of sales production that I was delivering! The production fell so quickly and finally that I was asked to come back on several occasions but I could never go back -only forward!

It bothered me greatly that white men could come into any black neighborhood and pick up the prettiest black girls and do whatever they wanted to and absolutely nothing could be done about it. History has always reflected much tolerance of the white man and the black woman, it was just like in the days of "Kings" ruling, no one can say no to a King, that's not the kind of King that I ever wanted to be, just in my family with all freedoms in place. The guy whose great grandfather was a slave owner and traded we'll call him WB, he was a quiet slim kind of wiry fellow and I guest he did all that he could to keep his secret a secret! Years later after middle age I had a general conversation with him during the time that I was visiting my home Church in Rains SC. He told me that he had found out that he had a twin brother that he had only met for the first time at Fort Jackson for the induction into the Army during the Vietnam war. I later surmised that his Grandfather had sold him off! The idea caused me to consider all of the relatives of mine who were sold all over the world. The slavery hangover is alive and well, slavery caused a great dis-connect in the black race that can never be corrected. Separated in Africa and then again many times in America. I thought about changing my last name many times but it would simply cause another dis-connect when my great grandchildren try to find me 500 years from now. This idea creates a dichotomy that will always exist. It upsets me each time I have buy a Passport to visit Africa and other Countries where my people live. My feelings about Africa are wonderful, there is beauty there that is unlike anywhere in the world and the space is precious. Being taken and separated from your brothers and sister is un imaginable.

Slavery has been imposed upon many races but none has been like the African. Too many layers and forms of mental and physical abuse. Generational trauma is an effect that never goes away it's always one thought away. I find that there is nothing to combat that feeling of "lost". The entire Continent of Africa was Colonized with the exclusion and exception of "ETHIOPIA" alone, first London England invaded the Country and was systematically repelled totally in 1868, 2000 soldiers were killed and 1000 were captured and confined. In the 1880's the Italians under Mussolini came to conquer and subdue but they forgot that Ethiopia has always been God's Country, Abraham was sent from UR in Iraq to take his family the Israelites to settle in Canaan- old name for Ethiopia. They thrashed the Italians completely and the Italians had modern weapons during world war two. England was defeated in two hours and Italy was defeated in a few more hours. Ethiopia has their own "Alphabet" and their own Churches, paved streets and Christianity was first established in Ethiopia through King Solomon's son Meneleke from his wife "The Queen of Sheba" during the year's visit and stay in Jerusalem. The "Holy of Holies-Moses ten Commandments was sent to Ethiopia by King Solomon with his son Meneleke. Although the white historians are still claiming that no one Knows where the Holy of Holies is.

Africa is the fastest growing Continent on Earth with six out of every ten individuals are under the age of twenty five and many European Countries are trying to gain a new foothold in Africa, mainly China who have limited space in which to house their Citizens to live. Africa has vast spaces of land and waterways and China is investing in the development of the rail system in Africa.

However the Africans are aware of the tricks and schemes of the past Colonization, "never again"!

Africa Before Slavery

When God created man in Africa, for about the first one thousand years there was only black skinned people, Adam lived for nine hundred and thirty years and God put in him (DNA) for all colors of people but there were first Black and Brown people. They did as God ask and went all over the Planet subduing the lands, they were the first in China as you can clearly see the first "BUDA" in a statue with braided hair! Russia, Germany all over Europe. Mansa Musa the richest man who ever lived from Mali and Timbuktu, King Solomon had so much wealth until it was un-countable. Mansa Musa sent ships all over the world loaded down with Builders, carvers and farmers to inhabit the lands and move back and forth at will. They came to America and lived in the West, California and build houses to dwell in, unlike the American Indians who didn't build anything-just worship the land that God made. Africans were always tribal with over two thousand languages which caused tribal wars with the conqueror taking prisoners but Africa had never had jails or prisons-no word for jail! So they sold and enslaved the captives but the men would always be a problem to indoctrinate. Then economy was a barter system of trade, cows and goats, sheep were the money, there was no need for money as currency until the white Brazilians came to trade and by and by the whites said we will take your war captives off your hands, here is some whisky and trinkets, blankets and such. And the slave trade begun in the fourteenth century shortly

197

after thirteen fifty when the "Gun" was invented. The Gun and Cannons made it easy to capture and Colonize Africans all over the Continent except "Ethiopia!

Europeans (Whites) taught their Children and grandchildren that black Africans were inferior and hung from trees with no close on which gave rise to brutal treatment of African slaves all over the world. You can just walk up to a slave and hit as hard as you could on his faces and there was absolutely nothing that a slave could do because he was the owners property to do with as you will. Practice your punching power on the face of a slave, the black women could not say "NO" to a slave owner because it would result in a terrible whipping and being sold as soon as they healed. The slave was at the complete mercy of the white slave owner for four hundred years and what is most annoying to understand is that they taught their children to hate the slave even before the civil war to make sure that the domineering treatment would be kept alive!

Now get this, anytime that a black slave went to the slave Master to get permission to marry the woman that he loves the slave master would give him his permission but the master would put the woman in a cabin alone and have sex with her until she becomes pregnant. This practice would create a sense of degradation in the man and the woman, you have a half white son or daughter from a white man and he was the first have sex with your new wife before you could do or say one thing. That child would get preferential treatment from the slave master father in plain sight of all other children creating division within the black family. The black husband had absolutely no authority in his own home because the house nor the woman belonged to him nor children! The white men told their children that they did the African slaves a big favor by bringing them to America to work and obey because in African they could possibly be eaten by other Africans.

The light skinned child from the white slave master is considered to be a sooner-not white and not black but a white man's creation, so in the white man's mind every time he sees a light skinned person he automatically knows that this is a white man's creation. It only took one drop of black blood to be a Nigger! Today we as African Americans expect to have to pay higher interest rates and go through more rigorous scrutiny when trying to purchase a house and car, we pay more than anyone else and we pay more for our food in grocery stores. Thursday, Friday, Saturday and Sunday because we get paid on Thursdays and Fridays the prices change on Wednesdays. Anytime a blue light flashes behind us on the highways we have to calm down from the instant fright and prepare ourselves for what could be deadly any day. We are still the first fired or laid off and promotions are tricky. Once when I was a kid about seven or eight years old my friend Lee and I went into a local convenience store which was owned by our community Sheriff, now you no the store that we normally went to sell our soda bottles and buy nick nacks, baby Ruth's Mary Janes, ice cream sandwiches etc., was a very likable friendly guy that's why everyone used to go there-James H. was his name. We just wanted to try this to see if he would pay us more for our bottles. This white fella was a tall big guy with a deep lazy sounding voice and each time we asked-ordered something he would say immediately-" What else" as if he was trying to get us to spend all of our money at his store! This man was never friendly or pleasant to be around I guest he felt like he had to always be intimidating since he was the Sheriff.

We never went back into that store and we found out why no one else did either, his attitude and his merchandise-candy was old and we knew that we couldn't take it back. The other store owner was right directly across the railroad tracks from Frank S. the Sheriff's store, he had everything-just like the Walmart is today and he made lots of money from black people. He wound up building a community nursing home which was a very positive thing for our people, black and whites could use it. One day my light skinned friend went into James H. Store and he ask my friend who his father was, this guy knew everyone in the community so when he told him who his father was he just looked at me and laughed. Looking back on those things now there was always a white owned General store in each black neighborhood, they made sure they got all of the black folk's money. Money from gathering Tobacco, picking cotton, braking corn and such. In the North there was nothing and hardly any jobs that young black teen agers could get during the Summer or winter. In the South we got to see beautiful blue jays and red birds, Robins and rice birds, I never saw a Blue Jay or red bird in New York. It is very important for me to know that I can always Go to Africa, my homeland of beauty. Although you have to carry your own money it is still good to know that I can always go Home, just like the Bible says, we would always come back home! It is going to be interesting when I go back and buy property and build a house, my old age home. Hopefully my grandchildren will give that idea some thought. There will always be change and change is something that I'm looking forward to, Africa is rising and I'd like to help. When our Cities and Communities become open again after Covid-19 It will be interesting to see how many people will continue to work from home-that's what I'm teaching now.

CHAPTER TWELVE

Black Originals-Called Black Indians

My great grandfather was half Cherokee Indian, however some of my earlier ancestors were captured already existing and during fine until they were captured after befriending the Europeans who came to our lands. For thousands of years the "Pequot" and many other tribes of Africans living, building and farming in this land that we now call America, they built their own houses with running water and stables for horses and mules. The Pequot black Indian tribe now living in the western part of the Country are still during fine, were never captured and enslaved-my family was and brought to South Carolina and other Southern states. During Slavery many of my family ran away and connected with the tribes called Moroons in Florida, they fought against the US Calvary and won for eight years. History will never tell that truth because the publishing house are controlled by whites! I read a book called Black Indians many years ago and I found some very interesting stuff! When the slaves escaped they did not keep the plantation owner's last name, instead they created names like "JOHN HORSE, AND WILD CAT" who are literally famous until this day. After defeating the Calvary, they went to Texas and Mexico to live and still fight on! It is very revealing and exhilarating to find nuggets during research about my people. When I was a very young boy I was told the truth by my Grandfather and I never had the displeasure of ever feeling inferior to anyone.

Black Indians

There was a full blood Indian or perhaps two thirds in my elementary school class-Harry P. did not look much different from many other brown skinned people that I knew in my lifetime- boy was very strong though but so was many other pure black people including my relatives. Many people in my family had great intuitive skills, they are very good at creating and making useful things which in find very useful today. These black Indians ventured into the military and wound up becoming talented cowboys working on ranches and cattle drives. There was one who became a very famous US MARSHALL, so did Fredrick Douglas. Bulldogging was invented by a black cowboy who was only 5'6, he developed a style of riding and roping cows from his horse -taking the animal by the horns and twisting its head until the nose was pointed towards the sky and biting the cow's nose until he could subdue him long enough to rope and tie all feet together. He holds records today for the fastest roping and tying cow's feet together. The Black cowboys knew the territory and the forested areas, the swamps and terrain as I wandered all over the woods in my hometown. I mentioned earlier that my friend Lee and made our own bows and arrows that would fly out of sight momentarily in the sky. I get very sad sometimes when I think about all of the rich and hardy History of my people that was not mentioned in any History books until this day. Instead we have obstacles to overcome at every hand and juncture to keep us in the dark. However there is tons of information in books in this and other Countries that I intend to find, I love to read and it is exhilarating to find knew information.

Black Cowboys

Many ex-slaves became renown and fierce cowboys as a way to make a substantial living both during and after the Civil War. Bill Pickett, the 5'6 inch rodeo performer who developed the "Bulldogging technique became world famous. The tenth of thirteen children and ten children of his own the rodeo was his way out of poverty. Bass Reeves was an outstanding brave Lawman-US Marshall who always got his man black and white, he didn't care where he had to go to get you or how long it took. He was well respected.

Black Life Today 2021

In the minds of black people today all over the world there is a Supreme suspicion of the white "Police".

Nothing has changed since the white slave catchers roamed this Country years ago. I don't personally live in fear but there is always that fear when I see the "Blue lights" behind me. It is very hard for me to understand that white people join the police force to get their opportunity to kill black and brown people. As in the Charleston shooting in the back of the un-armed black man running away from the police officer who yelled into his two-way radio "Tazer, Tazer, Tazer while he had his Tazer in his left hand while shooting the man in the back with his right hand. The video showed the officer then walk over to the man's dead body and clearly drop his Tazer down on the body of the dead man! It is very hard to understand the Humanity of the white police, White Supremacy has done a job on a lot of white people, even after we finally got a guilty verdict in court of "Chauvin" the officer who held his knee the neck of "George Floyd" almost ten minutes with his hands comfortably in his pockets. The entire world saw that and there can never be a denial of the murder! The very same week the Police killed black men and a young sixteen black girl. I have been preaching the fact that the "Police for was started for "Black people "free and enslaved in 1641 only twenty years after the first indentured black slaves got free in Jamestown Virginia from 1619 and went back to Charleston South Carolina. We saw on January 6, 2021 at the Capital building hundreds of white man and women storm the white House, beating and spraying Bear spray-a deadly chemical on the Police and they Police just stood there.

Today's Tragedies

And did nothing except take the punching, hitting with hard objects and sprayings, did not fight back at all and hardly any arrests. All of those Terrorist were simply allowed to do as they pleased without any consequences to excuse one woman who was jumping directly into the faces of the police and got shot! Only one gun shot and no arrests hardly. We absolutely never hear of the police shooting and killing a single white person no matter what they do except in the case of a mass shooting. The young white

"Dillan Roof" who shot the nine Church members of Mother Emanuel Church in Charleston South Carolina. When he was caught on his way to West Virginia the Police took him to "Burger King first to give him a Burger and fries, hard to imagine. Without out the aid of the cell phone videos we would be just like life was in the sixteen and seventeen hundreds. We can be killed simply because of the color of our skin any day!

American History omits-leaves absent the many feats and accomplishments of the African American, for instance-" THE ALAMO", many movies and much talk has permitted the conversations of events that occurred during the seige and battle of the Texas army when they were taking the owned land and property of the Mexicans in Mexico. There were hundreds of runaway slaves who migrated to Mexico under the name given them "moroons" who moved from Florida everglades and Seminole Indians. There was no "slavery" in Mexico so the black Cowboys-runaways joined the Mexican Army against Samuel Houston, Davey Crockett, Jim Bouwe who were slave owners who wanted to recapture Southern slaves and take the land of Mexico for America. There were only 250 combatants inside the Alamo-, old Spanish mission under the supervision of General Travis of the Texas army! Ultimately they were all slaughtered with the exception of one ex-slave "Joe", 49 other white women and children were allowed to survive to tell the story. The black cowboys were mostly in leadership roles in the Mexican army and fought gallantly in the defeat of the Texans. Texas and California was a part of Mexico and today Spanish speaking people are breaching the wall at the Mexican Border by the thousands every day! America is the only super power today but it is at the cost of ravishing all other small weaker Countries at their desire to have the commodities and products produced in those Countries. In the 1950" s America acquired Hawaii which produces various nuts, sugar cane, pineapples and such so America can purchase all very cheap. It is very unfortunate for the weak and the poor on the planet Earth, no escape to be left alone and in peace.

During the early seventeen and eighteenth Centuries in the Europe and America the "World bank" was established by the Rothchild family in Germany-his five sons were sent to various European Countries to establish Banking businesses in France, Austria, Portugal England and the United States of America. John D. Rockefeller, JP Morgan of Chase Manhattan Bank, the biggest bank in America. The Bush family is into oil. The Windsor family is also involved in the Richest families in the "world". JP Morgan developed "Wall street and the stock market which is the location of the largest "Slave market" in the world. New York was the largest Slave State at one time. Theas are untold and untaught truths that will never show up in any History books.

The Rothchild family funded the digging of the "Suez Canal" and renamed the "Holy Land" the "Middle east" which is still Egypt-African Land. The world bank funds wars-The English and the French, both sides, Iran and Iraq-both sides, whichever side will benefit the funding family will ultimately win. African cousins have been scattered all over the world just like the Bible says. Unfortunately when you are the weaker of two foes you wind up being Colonized and enslaved. The Continent of Africa has always been relatively easy to conquer because of the many Languages and Countries dilemma, however Africa is still the richest Continent on the Planet with twelve million miles of

"Land" and one point four Billion people, another Billion is spread over the 241 recognized Countries with a formal Government in place. Africans are not the minority in the world.

I am very proud of the strides of my people when I think and reflect globally, in France, Napoleon had five black Generals by his side. General Alexander Dumas was one of a magnificent statue of six feet two inches tall, was a great swordsman and warrior in all facets of war. The first three popes of Rome were "Black". Africans have the intrinsic innate ability to thrive under terrible circumstances and that history will never be printed in History books, it would not benefit the race currently in power. My thirst for knowledge is impeccable, I utilize my opportunities to self-educate myself for the rest of my life. To know that my people fought in all wars is phenomenal under the worst treatment possible. The world went to great lengths to keep us uneducated with no knowledge of our past. Very derogative scenes and statements were taught to me about Africa. We were only shown in books and the media the very worst of poor people and communities in Africa, however I've managed to discover the very best of Africa. Kilimanjaro the highest mountain in the world, "Lake Victoria" the highest waterfall in the world, although the Africans haven't accepted the Queen of England's Name. The mindset of a people who would go to extreme lengths to keep Africans in the dark about their original history in Egypt and Tinbutu, Senegal and Zimbabwe. Egypt gave the world the "second and Minute" in time. For a great many years the world tried to teach us that white people are responsible for all the great historical buildings in Egypt even though we always knew that only Africans are responsible for building and discoveries in Egypt. It was in just the last fifty years that scientist and archeologist have determined that all civilizations and people originated in Africa, the cradle of all civilization. We are the parents of all peoples of the Earth.

Many objects in the visual scenery in Africa, Military posts, statues of white colonizers who came, conquered and destroyed the pleasant serene atmosphere all over the Continent. 55 Countries with each using several languages which makes it easy to divide and conquer so all of the Europeans came and made handy work of subduing a people whose free living style of existing a mystical story in History. Everything was taken and flipped in the historical events of life. None of the other Island people had a developed civilization like the African so only the raw materials of value, exporting goods and such were taken. Of all inhabitants of the 241 Countries Africa is the richest that keep on giving and on top of that Africa has a vast Land mass of which China is investing money and business because China is overcrowded, no space for the one point five Billion people. They are still not allowing couples to have more than one child. However, it is a great help in the development of the African economy-if the Government officials keep their eyes open for the good of the Continent rather than filling their pockets and forgetting about the general welfare of the people.

CHAPTER THIRTEEN

Reflections Of The Past, Present And Future

When God made Adam in Ethiopia-as the whole of Africa was called in the beginning, God told Adam and his sons to subdue the "whole Earth" consequently they went and were the first to live in China, India, Rome -Italy, Germany, Netherlands, America, the "PEQUOT" people whom the Europeans named "Indians" as they did almost all of the indigenous peoples of the world. They built great magnificent building structures that the scientist today cannot figure out how and who built them! Human bones twenty seven million years old have been found in South Africa, and Historical writings have been discovered but the whites in power cannot afford to print that in History books of a people whom they brought to America to work for free and remain slaves "forever"...

When I was a student at Morris College it seems that I was always not of my choosing, connected to a girl whom I dated. There was a young girl, a dark skinned "beauty" from Greenville South Carolina that I called "JO" short for JO-ANN. It was my specific intention to put everyone else aside and make this Girl mine. Many nights when I lie down to sleep at night (today) I often think of things and events in my past that give me great pleasure before I fall asleep, as soon as I lie down I scan my mind for the thoughts that will make me happy and it's always the same thing that I left on the table-un-done. Perhaps my spirit is trying to educate me on my mistakes, this girl was without a doubt the most beautiful girl in the State which is much greater than the prettiest girl on Morris College Campus.

We all say and think of things that we wish that we would have done, however this is different, much stronger feelings than normal continue to take me back to seeing JO on the campus and in the Dining hall each day. So then, I can't explain it so I think of the metaphysical world where everything in life is forever. I have no idea how things will play out so I continue to think-not dream. Suppose there will be settings of alternating events throughout eternity. Suppose there will be different spaces in time to accommodate the thoughts that we build on while we are on Earth such that we travel to different mansions to live with total and complete happiness forever. As I understand it as soon as we transition we revert back to age 33 as the ancient scriptures explain the reason that Jesus chose to die at the age of 33. Everyone in the Kingdom will be age 33 forever, I certainly can imagine seeing the beautiful faces and bodies and that would make me extremely happy forever! I tried to contact JO but to no avail so I must leave the unknown in the invisible world of spirit.

There are many things in this Country that leaves me uncertain, when all of the unfortunate and untrue History unfolds as I know that it will we can stop living in this dream world that has been feed to us. Black people will be able to reclaim their African names and Culture. To live a life free of being exploited and mistreated by the Police daily. The Monetary system will not be controlled by a select few and money will not be dominating our minds daily. To be able to wake up every day thinking of someone to help along the way of life is very fulfilling to me. To watch the newborns come into our families continually. That is the way that is was in Africa before the white man came. God told Ham how to divide the land on Earth between his four sons but "greed" is very unfortunate-to much greed that is. It is a very good and profound law to not covet anything that is owned by your neighbor. The opposites of good and bad would be eliminated from existence!

Present

Overall life in America is uncertain at best. With the event at the Capital building in January 6, 2021 there was an unfolding of the mindset of many people which was not new, it just exploded to the open forefront. I'm often reminded when I daydream or reminisce that I was born in the very State that the Civil War was started in-Fort Sumter so it was nothing new, however I don't allow the thoughts to open up fully in my mind, the horrific treatment of my people in the past. I think and dwell on new possibilities to show up. Talking to "JO" now, we've come a long way and life is everlasting and I'm looking forward to it.

"Finally"

Being a scholar and historian, the founder of ON TTRACC BIBLE BUSINESS COLLEGE I find it delicate to discuss the "fact" to the world at large that "King James" of our Bible and the first King of England was "BLACK". He was also King of Scotland-King James the six, of Ireland as well-he was the son of a Black father and colored mother. I mentioned previously in this book that he hired fifty scholars to dissect and re-write the Holy Bible and make corrections.

I wish to thank DR. Robert Davidson a great teacher at our Bible College, and to Jo-ann Piles, look for my next book.

CONGRATULATIONS TO: PROF. DR. REV ROBERT DAVIDSON

Printed in the United States
by Baker & Taylor Publisher Services